LAWS AND LEGISLATION

RECREATIONAL AND MEDICAL MARIJUANA

LEGALIZATION CONFLICTS AND QUESTIONS

LAWS AND LEGISLATION

Additional books in this series can be found on Nova's website under the Series tab.

Additional E-books in this series can be found on Nova's website under the E-book tab.

LAWS AND LEGISLATION

RECREATIONAL AND MEDICAL MARIJUANA

LEGALIZATION CONFLICTS AND QUESTIONS

VALENTIN DIJKSTRA
EDITORS

New York

For permission to use material from this book please contact us:
Telephone 631-231-7269; Fax 631-231-8175
Web Site: http://www.novapublishers.com

Additional color graphics may be available in the e-book version of this book.

LIBRARY OF CONGRESS CATALOGING-IN-PUBLICATION DATA

ISBN: 978-1-62808-114-5

Published by Nova Science Publishers, Inc. † New York

CONTENTS

PREFACE

May a state authorize the use of marijuana for recreational purposes even if such use is forbidden by federal law? This novel and unresolved legal question has vexed judges, politicians, and legal scholars, and it has also generated considerable public debate among supporters and opponents of "legalizing" the recreational use of marijuana. This book summarizes the Washington and Colorado marijuana legalization laws and evaluates whether, or the extent to which, they may be preempted by the Controlled Substances Act (CSA) or by international agreements. It also highlights potential responses to these recent legalization initiatives by the U.S. Department of Justice (DOJ) and identifies other noncriminal consequences that marijuana users may face under federal law.

Chapter 1 – Under the federal Controlled Substances Act (CSA), the cultivation, distribution, and possession of marijuana are prohibited for any reason other than to engage in federally approved research. Yet 18 states and the District of Columbia currently exempt qualified users of medicinal marijuana from penalties imposed under state law. In addition, Colorado and Washington recently became the first states to legalize, regulate, and tax small amounts of marijuana for nonmedicinal (so-called "recreational") use by individuals over the age of 21. Thus, the current legal status of marijuana appears to be both contradictory and in a state of flux: as a matter of federal law, activities related to marijuana are generally prohibited and punishable by criminal penalties, whereas at the state level, certain marijuana usage is increasingly being permitted. Individuals and businesses engaging in marijuana-related activities that are authorized by state law nonetheless remain subject to federal criminal prosecution or other consequences under federal law.

The Colorado and Washington laws that legalize, regulate, and tax an activity the federal government expressly prohibits appear to be logically inconsistent with established federal policy toward marijuana, and are therefore likely subject to a legal challenge under the constitutional doctrine of preemption. This doctrine generally prevents states from enacting laws that are inconsistent with federal law. Under the Supremacy Clause, state laws that conflict with federal law are generally preempted and therefore void and without effect. Yet Congress intended that the CSA would not displace all state laws associated with controlled substances, as it wanted to preserve a role for the states in regulating controlled substances. States thus remain free to pass laws relating to marijuana, or any other controlled substance, so long as they do not create a "positive conflict" with federal law, such that the two laws "cannot consistently stand together."

This report summarizes the Washington and Colorado marijuana legalization laws and evaluates whether, or the extent to which, they may be preempted by the CSA or by international agreements. It also highlights potential responses to these recent legalization initiatives by the U.S. Department of Justice (DOJ) and identifies other noncriminal consequences that marijuana users may face under federal law. Finally, the report closes with a description of legislative proposals introduced in the 113th Congress relating to the treatment of marijuana under federal law, including H.R. 499 (Ending Federal Marijuana Prohibition Act of 2013); H.R. 501 (Marijuana Tax Equity Act of 2013); H.R. 689 (States' Medical Marijuana Patient Protection Act); H.R. 710 (Truth in Trials Act); H.R. 784 (States' Medical Marijuana Property Rights Protection Act); and H.R. 964 (Respect States' and Citizens' Rights Act of 2013).

Chapter 2 – As part of a larger scheme to regulate drugs and other controlled substances, federal law prohibits the cultivation, distribution, and possession of marijuana. No exception is made for marijuana used in the course of a recommended medical treatment. Indeed, by categorizing marijuana as a Schedule I drug under the Controlled Substances Act (CSA), the federal government has concluded that marijuana has "no currently accepted medical use in treatment in the United States." Yet 18 states and the District of Columbia have decriminalized medical marijuana by enacting exceptions to their state drug laws that permit individuals to grow, possess, or use marijuana for medicinal purposes. In contrast to the complete federal prohibition, these 19 jurisdictions see medicinal value in marijuana and permit the drug's use under certain circumstances.

Although the U.S. Supreme Court has established Congress's constitutional authority to enact the existing federal prohibition on marijuana, principles of federalism prevent the federal government from mandating that the states actively support or participate in enforcing the federal law. While state resources may be helpful in combating the illegal use of marijuana, Congress's ability to compel the states to enact similar criminal prohibitions, to repeal medical marijuana exemptions, or to direct state police officers to enforce the federal law remains limited by the Tenth Amendment.

Even if the federal government is prohibited from mandating that the states adopt laws supportive of federal policy, the constitutional doctrine of preemption generally prevents states from enacting laws that are inconsistent with federal law. Under the Supremacy Clause, state laws that conflict with federal law are generally preempted and therefore void. Courts, however, have not viewed the relationship between state and federal marijuana laws in such a manner, nor did Congress intend that the CSA displace all state laws associated with controlled substances. Instead, the relationship between the federal ban on marijuana and state medical marijuana exemptions must be considered in the context of two distinct sovereigns, each enacting separate and independent criminal regimes with separate and independent enforcement mechanisms, in which certain conduct may be prohibited under one sovereign and not the other. Although state and federal marijuana laws may be "logically inconsistent," a decision not to criminalize—or even to expressly decriminalize—conduct for purposes of the law within one sphere does nothing to alter the legality of that same conduct in the other sphere.

This report will review the federal government's constitutional authority to enact the federal criminal prohibition on marijuana; highlight certain principles of federalism that prevent the federal government from mandating that states participate in enforcing the federal prohibition; consider unresolved questions relating to the extent to which state authorization and regulation of medical marijuana are preempted by federal law; and assess what obligations, if any, the U.S. Department of Justice (DOJ) has to investigate and prosecute violations of the federal prohibition on marijuana.

Chapter 3 – This report highlights certain non-criminal regulatory requirements of the Controlled Substances Act (CSA). The CSA and its implementing regulations establish a framework through which the federal government regulates the use of controlled substances for legitimate medical, scientific, research, and industrial purposes, and prevents these substances from being diverted for illegal purposes. The CSA assigns various plants, drugs, and chemicals (such as narcotics, stimulants, depressants, hallucinogens, and anabolic steroids) to one of five schedules based on the substance's medical use, potential for abuse, and safety or dependence liability. Schedule I contains substances that have no currently accepted medical use and cannot safely be made available to the public under a prescription, while Schedules II, III, IV, and V include substances that have recognized medical uses and may be manufactured, distributed, and used in accordance with the CSA. The order of the schedules reflects substances that are progressively less dangerous and addictive. To restrict access to chemicals used in the illicit manufacture of certain controlled substances, the CSA also regulates 40 "listed chemicals." Furthermore, the CSA regulates controlled substance "analogues," which are substances that are not controlled but are structurally or pharmacologically similar to substances found in Schedule I or II and have no accepted medical use.

Unless specifically exempted by the CSA, any person who handles controlled substances or listed chemicals (such as drug manufacturers, wholesale distributors, doctors, hospitals, pharmacies, and scientific researchers) must register with the Drug Enforcement Administration (DEA) in the U.S. Department of Justice, which administers and enforces the CSA. Registrants must keep accurate and complete records of all transactions involving controlled substances, maintain detailed inventories of the substances in their possession, and periodically file reports with the DEA, as well as ensure that controlled substances are securely stored and safeguarded in accordance with DEA regulations.

Chapter 4 – This is a chart of the maximum fines and terms of imprisonment that may be imposed as a consequence of conviction for violation of the federal Controlled Substances Act (CSA) and other drug supply and drug demand related laws.

It lists the penalties for: heroin, cocaine, crack, PCP, LSD, marihuana (marijuana), amphetamine, methamphetamine, listed (precursor) chemicals, paraphernalia, date rape drugs, rave drugs, designer drugs, ecstasy, drug kingpins, as well as the other substances including narcotics and opiates assigned to Schedule I, Schedule II, Schedule III, Schedule IV, and Schedule V of the Controlled Substances Act and the Controlled Substances Import and Export Act (Title II and Title III of the Comprehensive Drug Abuse and Control Act).

It maps the penalty structure for violations of 21 U.S.C. 841 (drug trafficking), 21 U.S.C. 841(b)(5) (cultivation on federal property), 21 U.S.C. 841(b)(6) (environmental damage from illegal manufacturing), 21 U.S.C. 841(b)(7) (crime of violence), 21 U.S.C. 841(c) (offenses involving listed chemicals), 21 U.S.C. 841(d) (booby traps on federal lands), 21 U.S.C. 841(f) (distribution/possession of listed chemicals), 21 U.S.C. 841(g) (Internet sales of date rape drugs), 21 U.S.C. 841(h) (dispensing controlled substances that are prescription drugs by means of the Internet), 21 U.S.C. 842 (regulatory offenses), 21 U.S.C. 843 (communications-related offenses), 21 U.S.C. 844 (simple possession), 21 U.S.C. 846, 963 (attempt and conspiracy), 21 U.S.C. 849 (drug dealing at truck stops), 21 U.S.C. 848 (continuing criminal enterprises (CCE)), 21 U.S.C. 854, 855 (investment of illicit drug profits), 21 U.S.C. 856 (establishing manufacturing operations), 21 U.S.C. 858 (endangering human life), 21 U.S.C. 859 (distribution to infants, minors, children, juveniles, and those under 18 years of age), 21 U.S.C. 860 (distribution in school zones), 21 U.S.C. 861 (distribution to pregnant women), 21 U.S.C. 863 (trafficking in drug paraphernalia), 21 U.S.C. 864 (theft of anhydrous ammonia, or transportation of stolen anhydrous ammonia), 21 U.S.C. 865 (smuggling methamphetamine into the United States), 21 U.S.C. 960 (illicit drug import and export), 21 U.S.C. 960a (narco-terrorism), 21 U.S.C. 962 (recalcitrant drug smugglers), 21 U.S.C. 1906 (financial transactions with designated foreign narcotics traffickers), 18 U.S.C. 545 (smuggling goods into the United States), 18 U.S.C. 546 (smuggling goods into foreign countries), 18 U.S.C. 924(c) (firearms and armor piercing ammunition in connection to drug trafficking crime), 18 U.S.C. 924(e) (armed career criminals), 18 U.S.C. 1952 (Travel Act), 18 U.S.C. 1956 (money laundering), 18 U.S.C. 1957 (monetary transactions in property derived from unlawful activity), 18 U.S.C. 1959 (compensated crime of violence in aid of racketeering), 18 U.S.C. 1963 (racketeering (RICO)), 18 U.S.C. 2118 (robberies and burglaries involving controlled substances), 18 U.S.C. 3559(c) (three strikes), 19 U.S.C. 1590 (aviation smuggling), 26 U.S.C. 7201 (tax evasion), 26 U.S.C. 7203 (failure to file required returns), 26 U.S.C. 7206 (fraud and false statements), 31 U.S.C. 5322 (currency transaction reporting (smurfing)), 31 U.S.C. 5332 (bulk cash smuggling into or out of the United States), 46 U.S.C. 70506 (maritime drug law enforcement).

This report reflects amendments to the Controlled Substances Act made by the Fair Sentencing Act of 2010 (P.L. 111-220) that increased the quantities of crack cocaine necessary to trigger certain penalties and also increased the fine amounts for major drug traffickers.

In: Recreational and Medical Marijuana
Editors: Valentin Dijkstra
ISBN: 978-1-62808-114-5

Chapter 1

STATE LEGALIZATION OF RECREATIONAL MARIJUANA: SELECTED LEGAL ISSUES*

Todd Garvey and Brian T. Yeh

SUMMARY

May a state authorize the use of marijuana for recreational purposes even if such use is forbidden by federal law? This novel and unresolved legal question has vexed judges, politicians, and legal scholars, and it has also generated considerable public debate among supporters and opponents of "legalizing" the recreational use of marijuana.

Under the federal Controlled Substances Act (CSA), the cultivation, distribution, and possession of marijuana are prohibited for any reason other than to engage in federally approved research. Yet 18 states and the District of Columbia currently exempt qualified users of medicinal marijuana from penalties imposed under state law. In addition, Colorado and Washington recently became the first states to legalize, regulate, and tax small amounts of marijuana for nonmedicinal (so-called "recreational") use by individuals over the age of 21. Thus, the current legal status of marijuana appears to be both contradictory and in a state of flux: as a matter of federal law, activities related to marijuana are generally prohibited and punishable by criminal penalties, whereas at the state level, certain marijuana usage is increasingly being

* This is an edited, reformatted and augmented version of the Congressional Research Service Publication, CRS Report for Congress R43034, dated April 5, 2013.

permitted. Individuals and businesses engaging in marijuana-related activities that are authorized by state law nonetheless remain subject to federal criminal prosecution or other consequences under federal law.

The Colorado and Washington laws that legalize, regulate, and tax an activity the federal government expressly prohibits appear to be logically inconsistent with established federal policy toward marijuana, and are therefore likely subject to a legal challenge under the constitutional doctrine of preemption. This doctrine generally prevents states from enacting laws that are inconsistent with federal law. Under the Supremacy Clause, state laws that conflict with federal law are generally preempted and therefore void and without effect. Yet Congress intended that the CSA would not displace all state laws associated with controlled substances, as it wanted to preserve a role for the states in regulating controlled substances. States thus remain free to pass laws relating to marijuana, or any other controlled substance, so long as they do not create a "positive conflict" with federal law, such that the two laws "cannot consistently stand together."

This report summarizes the Washington and Colorado marijuana legalization laws and evaluates whether, or the extent to which, they may be preempted by the CSA or by international agreements. It also highlights potential responses to these recent legalization initiatives by the U.S. Department of Justice (DOJ) and identifies other noncriminal consequences that marijuana users may face under federal law. Finally, the report closes with a description of legislative proposals introduced in the 113th Congress relating to the treatment of marijuana under federal law, including H.R. 499 (Ending Federal Marijuana Prohibition Act of 2013); H.R. 501 (Marijuana Tax Equity Act of 2013); H.R. 689 (States' Medical Marijuana Patient Protection Act); H.R. 710 (Truth in Trials Act); H.R. 784 (States' Medical Marijuana Property Rights Protection Act); and H.R. 964 (Respect States' and Citizens' Rights Act of 2013).

INTRODUCTION

Supreme Court Justice Louis Brandeis famously praised the division of sovereign powers included within America's constitutional structure for its capacity to encourage states to "serve as a laboratory; and try novel social and economic experiments without risk to the rest of the country."[1] This legislative freedom is constrained, however, by various constitutional restrictions including the Supremacy Clause, which provides that federal law "shall be the supreme Law of the Land."[2] Pursuant to this established principle of federal legal preeminence, any state law that conflicts with federal law is generally considered preempted and therefore void. Although simple in theory, the task of determining whether a state law is "in conflict" with federal law can be incredibly complex in practice.

The ongoing national debate over marijuana provides a clear example of the confusion associated with the states' ability to pursue policies that deviate from those advanced by the federal government. In addition to the 18 states and the District of Columbia that currently exempt qualified users of medicinal marijuana[3] from penalties imposed under state law, Colorado and Washington recently became the first states to legalize,[4] regulate, and tax small amounts of marijuana for personal (i.e., nonmedicinal) use by individuals over the age of 21.[5] These broad legalization initiatives stand in stark contrast to federal law, which makes the cultivation, distribution, or possession of any amount of marijuana—for any purpose other than bona fide, federally approved scientific research—a criminal offense.[6]

Therefore, the possession, cultivation, or distribution of marijuana remains a *federal* crime within Colorado, Washington, and every other state. As a result, individuals who grow, possess, use, sell, transport, or distribute marijuana, even when done in a manner consistent with state law or pursuant to a state-issued license, are nonetheless in violation of the federal Controlled Substances Act (CSA) and remain subject to federal criminal prosecution or other consequences under federal law. Given the federal government's continued ability to enforce its own prohibition, it cannot be said that the Washington and Colorado laws create a right to use marijuana. Nor does compliance with state law provide a defense to a prosecution brought under federal law.[7] However, the extent to which federal authorities will actually seek to prosecute individuals who are engaged in marijuana-related activities in Colorado and Washington remains uncertain. President Obama himself has suggested that prosecuting simple possession is not a priority, while the Department of Justice (DOJ) has said only that "growing, selling, or possessing any amount of marijuana remains illegal under federal law."[8] A formal response from the DOJ is expected imminently.[9]

WASHINGTON INITIATIVE 502

Washington Initiative 502 legalizes marijuana possession by amending state law to provide that the possession of small amounts of marijuana "is not a violation of this section, this chapter, or any other provision of Washington law."[10] Under the Initiative, individuals over the age of 21 may possess up to one ounce of dried marijuana, 16 ounces of marijuana infused product in solid form, or 72 ounces of marijuana infused product in liquid form.[11] However, marijuana must be used in private, as it is unlawful to "open a package containing marijuana ... or consume marijuana ... in view of the general public."[12]

In addition to legalizing possession, the Initiative provides that the "possession, delivery, distribution, and sale" by a validly licensed producer, processor, or retailer, in accordance with the newly established regulatory scheme administered by the state Liquor Control Board (LCB), "shall not be a criminal or civil offense under Washington state law."[13] The Initiative establishes a three-tiered production, processing, and retail licensing system that permits the state to retain regulatory control over the commercial life cycle of marijuana. Qualified individuals must obtain a producer's license to grow or cultivate marijuana, a processor's license to process, package, and label the drug, or a retail license to sell marijuana to the general public.[14] The Initiative establishes various restrictions and requirements for obtaining the proper license and directs the state LCB to adopt procedures for the issuance of such licenses by December 1, 2013.[15] The LCB is authorized to promulgate additional implementing regulations, including rules controlling the total number of marijuana retailers in each county, labeling restrictions, security requirements for marijuana facilities, and reasonable time, place, and manner advertising restrictions.[16] In preparing to meet the December 1 deadline, the LCB has held eight public forums across the state to obtain public input on draft regulations.

Under the Initiative, the state will also impose an excise tax of 25% of the selling price on each marijuana sale within the established distribution system.[17] The state excise tax will, therefore, be imposed on three separate transactions: the sale of marijuana from producer to processor, from processor to retailer, and from retailer to consumer. All collected taxes are deposited into the Dedicated Marijuana Fund and distributed, mostly to social and health services, as outlined in the Initiative.[18]

The Initiative also specifically provides that operation of a motor vehicle while under the influence of marijuana remains a crime.[19]

COLORADO AMENDMENT 64

Unlike the relatively specific Initiative 502, Colorado Amendment 64 provides only a general framework for the legalization, regulation, and taxation of marijuana in Colorado—leaving regulatory implementation to the Colorado Department of Revenue.

Amendment 64 amends the Colorado Constitution to ensure that it "shall not be an offense under Colorado law or the law of any locality within Colorado" for an individual 21 years of age or older to possess, use, display, purchase, consume, or transport one ounce of marijuana; or possess, grow, process, or transport up to six marijuana plants.[20] Unlike Initiative 502, which permits only state-licensed facilities to grow marijuana, Amendment 64 allows any individual over the age of 21 to grow small amounts of marijuana for personal use.[21] Marijuana may not, however, be consumed "openly and publicly or in a manner that endangers others."[22]

In addition, the new law also provides that it shall not be unlawful for a marijuana-related facility to purchase, manufacture, cultivate, process, transport, or sell larger quantities of marijuana so long as the facility obtains a current and valid state-issued license.[23] Amendment 64 appears to envision a three-tier distribution and regulatory system, similar to that established in Washington, involving the licensing of marijuana cultivation facilities, marijuana product manufacturing facilities, and retail marijuana stores.[24] The Department of Revenue is directed to adopt regulations to implement licensing qualifications and procedures for these facilities not later than July 1, 2013, and to begin accepting license applications by October 1, 2013.[25] The Department must establish procedures for the issuance, renewal, suspension, and revocation of licenses; a schedule of licensing and renewal fees; and license qualifications including physical security, labeling, health and safety, and advertising requirements.[26]

Amendment 64 also mandates that the General Assembly enact an excise tax on the sale of marijuana by marijuana facilities that initially does not exceed 15%.[27] The first $40 million raised by the marijuana excise tax is to be credited to the Public School Capital Construction Assistance Fund.

Amendment 64 also ensures that employers are not required to accommodate the use of marijuana in the workplace and that driving under the influence of marijuana remains unlawful.[28]

Final Report of the Amendment 64 Implementation Task Force

Following approval of Amendment 64 by Colorado voters, Governor John Hickenlooper established the Amendment 64 Implementation Task Force (Task Force) to "identify the legal, policy and procedural issues that need to be resolved, and to offer suggestions and proposals ... that need to be taken" to effectively implement Amendment 64.[29] The Task Force issued a final report on March 13, 2013, consisting of 58 recommendations. Of those recommendations, the most significant include establishing a "vertical integration" model in which "cultivation, processing and manufacturing, and retail sales must be a common enterprise under common ownership";[30] imposing the required 15% excise tax while preserving the option for a future marijuana sales tax;[31] restricting commercial licenses to grow, process, or sell marijuana to state residents only;[32] and permitting both residents and nonresidents to purchase marijuana, but imposing more restrictive limits on the quantity of marijuana that may be purchased by out-of- state consumers.[33]

The Task Force recommendations remain advisory until implemented by either state law or administrative action.

FEDERAL LAW

Congress enacted the Controlled Substances Act (CSA)[34] as Title II of the Comprehensive Drug Abuse Prevention and Control Act of 1970.[35] The purpose of the CSA is to regulate and facilitate the manufacture, distribution, and use of controlled substances for legitimate medical, scientific, research, and industrial purposes, and to prevent these substances from being diverted for illegal purposes. The CSA places various plants, drugs, and chemicals (such as narcotics, stimulants, depressants, hallucinogens, and anabolic steroids) into one of five schedules based on the substance's medical use, potential for abuse, and safety or dependence liability;[36] Schedule I substances are deemed to have no currently accepted medical use in treatment and can only be used in very limited circumstances, whereas substances classified in Schedules II, III, IV, and V have recognized medical uses and may be manufactured, distributed, and used in accordance with the CSA. The CSA requires persons who handle controlled substances (such as drug manufacturers, wholesale distributors, doctors, hospitals, pharmacies, and scientific researchers) to register with the Drug Enforcement Administration (DEA) in the U.S. Department of Justice, the federal agency that administers and enforces the CSA.[37] Such registrants are subject to strict requirements regarding drug security, recordkeeping, reporting and production quotas, in order to minimize theft and diversion.[38] Federal civil and criminal penalties are available for anyone who manufactures, distributes, imports, or possesses controlled substances in violation of the CSA (both "regulatory" offenses as well as illicit drug trafficking and possession).[39]

Because controlled substances classified as Schedule I drugs have "a high potential for abuse" with "no currently accepted medical use in treatment in the United States" and lack "accepted safety for use of the drug [] under medical supervisions,"[40] doctors may not prescribe them to patients, and such substances may only be used for bona fide, federal government-approved research studies.[41] Under the CSA, only DEA-licensed doctors are allowed to prescribe controlled substances listed in Schedules II-V to patients.[42] Federal regulations stipulate that a lawful prescription for a controlled substance may only be "issued for a legitimate medical purpose by an individual practitioner acting in the usual course of his professional practice."[43]

The CSA establishes an administrative mechanism for substances to be controlled (added to a schedule); decontrolled (removed from the scheduling framework altogether); and rescheduled or transferred from one schedule to another.[44] Federal rulemaking proceedings to add, delete, or change the schedule of a drug or substance may be initiated by the DEA, the U.S. Department of Health and Human Services (HHS), or by petition by any interested person.[45] Congress may also change the scheduling status of a drug or substance through legislation.

When Congress enacted the CSA in 1970, marijuana was classified as a Schedule I drug.[46] Today, marijuana is still categorized as a Schedule I controlled substance and is therefore subject to the most severe restrictions contained within the CSA. Pursuant to the CSA, the unauthorized cultivation, distribution, or possession of marijuana is a federal crime.[47] Although various factors contribute to the ultimate sentence received, the mere possession of marijuana generally constitutes a misdemeanor subject to up to one year imprisonment and a minimum fine of $1,000.[48] A violation of the federal "simple possession" statute that occurs after a single prior conviction under any federal or state drug law triggers a mandatory minimum fine of $2,500 and a minimum imprisonment term of 15 days (up to a maximum of two years); if the defendant has multiple prior drug offense convictions at the time of his or her federal simple possession offense, the sentencing court must impose a mandatory minimum fine of $5,000 and a mandatory minimum imprisonment term of 90 days (up to a maximum term of three years).[49] On the other hand, the cultivation or distribution of marijuana, or the possession of marijuana with the intent to distribute is subject to more severe penalties. Such conduct generally constitutes a felony subject to as much as five years imprisonment and a fine of up to $250,000.[50]

FEDERAL PREEMPTION OF STATE LAW

The Colorado and Washington laws, which legalize, regulate, and tax an activity the federal government expressly prohibits, appear to be logically inconsistent with established federal policy and are therefore likely subject to a legal challenge under the constitutional doctrine of preemption. The principal that states cannot enact laws that contradict federal law is grounded in the Supremacy Clause of Article VI, cl. 2, which states that "[t]he Constitution, and the Laws of the United States which shall be made in Pursuance thereof; and all Treaties made ... under the Authority of the United States, shall be the supreme Law of the Land."[51] The Supremacy Clause, therefore, "elevates" the U.S. Constitution, federal statutes, federal regulations, and treaties[52] above the laws of the states.[53] As a result, where federal and state law are in conflict, the state law is generally preempted, leaving it void and without effect.[54]

The Supreme Court has established three general classes of preemption: express preemption, conflict preemption, and field preemption.[55] Express preemption exists where the language of a federal statute explicitly states the degree to which related state laws are superseded by federal law.[56] In contrast, where Congress does not articulate its view as to a statute's intended impact on state laws, a court may *imply* preemption if there is evidence that Congress intended to supplant state authority.[57] Preemption is generally implied in two situations. First, under field preemption, a state law is preempted where a "scheme of federal regulation is so pervasive as to make reasonable the inference that Congress left no room for the States to supplement it.... "[58] Second, under conflict preemption, a state law is preempted "where compliance with both federal law and state regulations is a physical impossibility ... *or* where state law stands as an obstacle to the accomplishment and execution of the full purposes and objectives of Congress."[59]

Regardless of the type of preemption at play, the task of evaluating the preemptive effect of a federal law is "one of determining congressional intent."[60] By making its intent clear, Congress may choose to preempt all related state laws, no state laws, or only select state laws.

Preemption under the Controlled Substances Act

In Section 708 of the CSA (21 U.S.C. §903), Congress specifically articulated the degree to which federal law was to preempt state controlled substances laws. This *express* preemption[61] provision recites language that evokes the principles of *conflict* preemption, stating,

> No provision of this subchapter shall be construed as indicating an intent on the part of the Congress to occupy the field in which that provision operates, including criminal penalties, to the exclusion of any State law on the same subject matter which would otherwise be within the authority of the State, *unless there is a positive conflict between that provision of this subchapter and that State law so that the two cannot consistently stand together*.[62]

Notably, the provision clarifies that Congress did not intend to entirely occupy the regulatory field concerning controlled substances or wholly supplant traditional state authority in the area. Indeed, Congress expressly declined to assert *field* preemption as grounds for preempting state law under the CSA. The Supreme Court has stated that this provision suggests that Congress "explicitly contemplate[d] a role for the States in regulating controlled substances."[63] As such, the preemptive effect of the CSA is not as broad as congressional authority could have allowed. States remain free to pass laws relating to marijuana, or other controlled substances, so long as they do not create a "positive conflict" with federal law, such that the two laws "cannot consistently stand together." In attempting to give effect to Congress's intent, courts have generally established that a state law is in "positive conflict" with the CSA only if

1. it is "physically impossible" to comply with both the state and federal law (the "impossibility prong"); or
2. the state law "stands as an obstacle to the accomplishment and execution of the full purposes and objectives of Congress."[64] (the "obstacle prong")

By preempting only those state laws in "positive conflict" with the CSA, without including any reference to those state laws that pose an obstacle to the CSA, some lower California courts have held that Congress did not intend 21 U.S.C. §903 to preempt state laws under the obstacle prong.[65] However, in 2009, the Supreme Court applied both the impossibility and obstacle prongs in interpreting the preemptive effect of a similar preemption provision found within the Food Drug and Cosmetic Act (FDCA).[66] That provision provided that a state law would be preempted only where it was in "direct and positive conflict" with federal law.[67] Given that most lower courts have applied both the impossibility and the obstacle prong in determining whether state medical marijuana laws are in "positive conflict" with the CSA, and the Supreme Court's recent interpretation of the FDCA preemption provision, it would appear that the preemptive effect of §903 likely extends to both those state laws that make it impossible to comply with federal law and those that create an obstacle to the accomplishment of Congress's objectives.

Although applicable, courts have only rarely invalidated a state law as preempted under the impossibility prong of the positive conflict test.[68] Under the generally adopted reasoning, unless state law *requires* what federal law *prohibits*, or state law *prohibits* what federal law *requires*, it is not "impossible" to comply with both laws.[69] In the medical marijuana context, for example, courts have generally asserted that an individual can comply with the CSA and a state medical marijuana exemption by refraining from the use of marijuana altogether.[70] As a general matter, it is clear that the principle provisions of the Colorado and Washington laws do not *require* individuals to engage in activity prohibited by federal law, and thus likely do not make it physically impossible to comply with both federal and state law.[71]

Given the narrowness with which courts have interpreted the first prong of the positive conflict test, the validity of state laws that appear inconsistent with federal law has traditionally hinged on whether the state law "stands as an obstacle to the accomplishment and execution of the full purposes and objectives of Congress. " Most of the following analysis, then, will focus on whether the Washington and Colorado laws represent such an obstacle.

Application of Preemption Principles to Washington and Colorado Legalization Measures

The extent to which a state law that legalizes, regulates, and taxes marijuana for recreational purposes may be preempted by the CSA is a novel and unresolved legal question. The federal courts, for instance, have not engaged in any substantial analysis of whether federal law preempts state marijuana laws.[72] Existing applicable precedent, which has arisen as a result of challenges to state *medical* marijuana laws, has been developed almost exclusively by state courts, and even then, mostly by lower court decisions that range widely in their approach to the preemption question.[73] This divergent body of precedent, in conjunction with the general preemption principles previously outlined, would appear to be the most likely source for the standards upon which the validity of the Washington and Colorado laws may be judged.

Before proceeding, it is important to note the structural similarities of both the Washington and Colorado laws. Each law seeks to achieve three different but interrelated objectives: the legalization of marijuana, the regulation and licensing of marijuana producers, processors, and retailers, and the taxation of marijuana sales. Because each of these objectives conflicts with federal law to a different degree, for purposes of a preemption analysis each aspect of the state laws must be considered separately.

At the outset, however, it is important to emphasize "two cornerstones of pre-emption jurisprudence," that will likely play a significant role in any review of the Washington or Colorado laws.[74] First, "the purpose of Congress is the ultimate touchstone in every pre-emption case."[75] Thus, in considering the preemptive scope of the CSA, it is necessary to establish Congress's "purpose" in enacting the law. The Supreme Court has previously identified the "main objectives" of the CSA as "conquer[ing] drug abuse" and "control[ing] the legitimate and illegitimate traffic in controlled substances."[76] Second, "[i]n all pre-emption cases ... we 'start with the assumption that the historic police powers of the States were not to be superseded by [federal law] unless that was the clear and manifest purpose of Congress."[77] State drug laws, including those connected to marijuana cultivation, distribution, or possession have generally been considered to be within "the historic police powers of the States."[78] Consequently, the Washington and Colorado laws would likely be accorded a presumption of validity.

Legalization

Both Colorado and Washington have provided that the possession of marijuana in accordance with certain restrictions[79] shall not be a violation of state law. It would appear unlikely that these aspects of both state laws—which only exempt certain individuals who possess marijuana from penalties under state law—would be preempted by federal law. It is important to reiterate however, that even if otherwise valid, permitting the possession, distribution or production of marijuana under state law does not alter the fact that the conduct remains a crime under federal law.

Under the police power, states are generally free to criminalize any conduct (within the bounds of state and federal constitutional protections) which they wish to deter.[80] Although the federal government may use its power of the purse to encourage states to adopt certain criminal laws, the federal government is limited in its ability to directly influence state policy by the Tenth Amendment, which prevents the federal government from directing states to enact specific legislation, or requiring state officials to enforce federal law.[81] As such, the fact that the federal government has criminalized conduct does not mean that the state, in turn, must also criminalize or prosecute that same conduct. It has generally been recognized that the states and the federal government operate as two distinct sovereigns, enacting separate and independent criminal regimes with separate and independent enforcement mechanisms, in which certain conduct may be prohibited under one sovereign and not the other.[82] If prohibiting certain conduct under federal law had the effect of barring any state attempt to permit that same conduct, the result would be a legal environment in which states were compelled to adopt criminal measures that mirrored federal law. The Tenth Amendment prohibits such a requirement.[83] In situations where states are unwilling to voluntarily prohibit conduct that Congress has determined should be deterred "the proper response—according to [the Tenth Amendment]—is to ratchet up the *federal* regulatory regime, *not* to commandeer that of the state."[84]

These principles of federalism would appear to both inform and restrict the reach of federal preemption. Under both Tenth Amendment and preemption principles, federal and state courts have previously held that a state's decision to simply *permit* what the federal government *prohibits* does not create a "positive conflict" with federal law.[85] As discussed above, under the impossibility prong of conflict preemption, the Supreme Court has specifically held that so long as an individual is not compelled by state law to engage in conduct prohibited by federal law, then simultaneous compliance with both laws is not "impossible."[86]

Nor have courts generally found that simply permitting conduct that the federal government prohibits stands as an "obstacle to the execution of Congress's objectives." The Supreme Court has interpreted this prong relatively narrowly, holding that a state law is preempted where the obstacle is of such a degree that "the purpose of the [federal] act cannot otherwise be accomplished."[87] In the medical marijuana context, courts have generally found that exempting individuals from state penalties has only a limited impact on the federal government's ability to combat the use of marijuana because an exemption under *state law* does not obstruct the federal government's ability to investigate and prosecute violations of *federal law.* It is well established that compliance with state medical marijuana laws is no defense, and provides no immunity to a federal criminal prosecution under the CSA.[88] The federal government remains free to expend its own resources to implement and enforce its own law, regardless of whether the state chooses to criminalize that same conduct. The fact that a state does not wish to expend its resources to implement a policy similar to that of the federal government, though likely making overall enforcement less effective,[89] has not, in the past, created an obstacle to the federal law sufficient to trigger preemption.[90]

In light of this dynamic, it would appear that those aspects of the Colorado and Washington laws that remove state penalties for possession of marijuana may properly be characterized as an exercise of the state's "power to decide what is criminal and what is not."[91] Neither law purports to shield its residents from the legal consequences of violating federal law. Given both the limitations on congressional power imposed by the Tenth Amendment and preemption precedent arising from challenges to state medical marijuana laws, it would appear unlikely that a reviewing court would invalidate either Colorado or Washington's decision to simply exempt certain marijuana-related conduct from state penalties under state law.

Regulation and Licensing

Although the legalization aspects of both the Washington and Colorado laws would likely survive a legal challenge, the regulation and licensing aspects of each law may raise more substantial preemption concerns. In addition to removing state penalties relating to certain marijuana-related activities, both states envision comprehensive, state implemented regulatory and licensing regimes to control the cultivation, distribution and sale of marijuana within the state. These provisions can arguably be distinguished from the legalization provisions in two key ways, both of which appear to support a finding of preemption. First, the regulatory and licensing provisions potentially create an increased "obstacle" to the accomplishment of federal objectives by "authorizing" conduct federal law prohibits. Second, the affirmative act of regulating and licensing marijuana cultivation and distribution may not invoke the same Tenth Amendment protections enjoyed by the states' initial decision to simply remove marijuana-related penalties under state law.

To the contrary, arguments can also be made in opposition to preemption. The regulation and licensing provisions could be viewed as a necessary implementation mechanism through which the states may efficiently identify those individuals who have met the requirements of the state marijuana law without impeding the enforcement of federal law. Moreover, the regulatory and licensing provisions could be characterized as imposing additional *restrictions* on marijuana access—an objective consistent with the purposes of the CSA—and thus are not subject to conflict preemption. These contrasting views, either of which could be invoked in a court's review of the Colorado and Washington laws, are discussed in greater detail below.

The Exemption/Authorization Distinction in Obstacle Preemption

Where the federal government has prohibited specific conduct, the Supreme Court appears to have expressed concern over state laws that go beyond exempting that conduct from state penalties, and instead attempt to actively "authorize" conduct in violation of federal law. In *Michigan Canners & Freezers v. Agricultural Board*, the Court held that a state law that permitted a state board to authorize a food producers association to act as an exclusive bargaining agent for all producers of a certain commodity was in conflict with a federal law that prohibited associations from interfering with an individual food producer's decision to sell its products on its own or through an association.[92] The Court determined that although it was possible to simultaneously comply with both the federal and state law, because the state board was empowered to "*authorize[]* producers' associations to engage in conduct that the federal act forbids, it 'stands as an obstacle to the accomplishment and execution of the full purposes and objectives of Congress.'"[93] Although the Court did not adopt an express distinction, the possibility that state "authorizations" may create a more substantial obstacle to the accomplishment of federal objectives than a state "exemption" from state penalties, could play a significant role in a court's evaluation of the Colorado and Washington laws.

Consider, for example, the Oregon Supreme Court decision in *Emerald Steel Fabricators v. Bureau of Labor and Industries*.[94] In that case the Oregon Supreme Court heard a challenge to the state identification card provisions of the Oregon Medical Marijuana Act. Under Oregon law, the state issued identification cards that permitted qualified individuals to "engage in the medical use … of marijuana" without the threat of state prosecution.[95] In evaluating the state law, the Oregon Supreme Court first affirmed that it was not invalidating Oregon's decision to simply exempt medical marijuana users from criminal liability under state law—suggesting that such measures were within the states' authority and beyond the reach of Congress under the Tenth Amendment.[96] The licensing provisions, however, which authorized an individual with an identification card to engage in the use of marijuana, were distinguishable.[97] The Court held that by "affirmatively authorizing a use that federal law prohibits," the Oregon law stood "as an obstacle to the implementation and execution of the full purposes and objectives of the Controlled Substances Act, " and was therefore preempted.[98] "[T]here is no dispute," the court concluded, "that Congress has the authority under the Supremacy Clause to preempt state laws that affirmatively authorize the use of medical marijuana."[99]

Most California courts, however, have not adopted the exemption/authorization distinction, and have instead generally upheld California medical marijuana identification card provisions. These cases have generally stressed that the Tenth Amendment protects California's decision to permit medicinal marijuana and that the state's medical marijuana law in no way affects the federal government's ability to prosecute for violations of federal law. For example, in *County of San Diego v. San Diego NORML*, and *Qualified Patients Association v. City of Anaheim*, an intermediate California appellate court twice upheld the identification card provisions of the California Medical Marijuana Program Act (MMPA).[100] Like the Oregon law, the MMPA provides that persons with valid identification cards shall not be subject to criminal sanctions under state law.

In both cases, the California appellate court held that the state law did not impose a significant obstruction to the federal objectives embodied within the CSA.[101] In *County of San Diego*, the court relied principally on a determination that the identification cards did not "insulate the bearer from federal laws," nor did the card "imply the holder is immune from prosecution for federal offenses."[102] The identification cards, the court reasoned, instead represented a "mechanism" by which California law enforcement officers could efficiently identify those individuals who are exempt from prosecution under California law for possessing marijuana.[103] In *Qualified Patients*, the court relied more heavily on the Supreme Court's statement in *Crosby v. National Foreign Trade Council*[104] that a state law presents a sufficient obstacle to the accomplishment of federal objectives only where "the purpose of the [federal] act cannot otherwise be accomplished," as well as the anti-commandeering principles of the Tenth Amendment.[105] In determining that the state law did not create a sufficient conflict with federal law, the court noted that "preemption theory [] is not a license to commandeer state or local resources to achieve federal objectives."[106]

However, in a ruling that was later dismissed as moot by the California Supreme Court after the city ordinance in question was repealed, one California appellate court deviated from *County of San Diego* and *Qualified Patients* in striking down a marijuana regulatory scheme that had been implemented by the City of Long Beach, California. *Pack v. City of Long Beach* involved a preemption challenge to a city ordinance that established a "comprehensive regulatory scheme by which medical marijuana collectives" were to be governed.[107] Pursuant to the ordinance, the city issued permits to marijuana collectives and adopted regulations that restricted their operation. In applying the obstacle prong to determine whether the local ordinance was preempted by the CSA,[108] the court clearly addressed the exemption/authorization distinction, reasoning that "there is a distinction, in law, between not making an activity unlawful and making the activity lawful ... The state law does not present an obstacle to Congress's purposes simply by not criminalizing conduct that Congress has criminalized."[109] However, the court concluded that the city ordinance "goes beyond decriminalization into authorization."[110] By establishing a permit scheme that "determines which collectives are permissible and which collectives are not," the city was affirmatively authorizing individuals to engage in conduct barred by federal law.[111] Citing *Michigan Canners*, the court held that such an action "'stands as an obstacle to the accomplishment and execution of the full purposes and objectives of Congress' and is therefore preempted."[112]

In light of these varying approaches, it is apparent that the extent to which state marijuana provisions (whether medicinal or recreational) are preempted by the CSA is unsettled. However, if a reviewing court were to adopt the exemption/authorization distinction applied in *Emerald Steel* and *Pack*, it would appear that the Colorado and Washington recreational licensing provisions would likely be invalidated. Both state initiatives involve a significantly higher degree of state involvement in the "authorizing" of marijuana activities than merely issuing identification cards. Both Colorado and Washington plan to implement a robust and comprehensive regulatory distribution scheme (akin to the ordinance at issue in *Pack*) that provides state issued licenses to marijuana producers, processors, and retailers.[113] An individual who obtains the proper license from the state would be *authorized* to grow, transport, or sell marijuana under state law. This licensing of marijuana-related activities by the state could be viewed as exceeding a decision to determine what conduct constitutes an offense under state law, and instead representing an action by the state to "affirmatively authorize" conduct prohibited under federal law.[114]

In the alternative, a reviewing court could adopt a line of reasoning similar to that in *County of San Diego* and *Qualified Patients* and determine that the Colorado and Washington licensing provisions are a proper exercise of state power and not in conflict with the CSA.[115] Under this reasoning, it can be argued that the state regulatory and licensing laws have no impact on the enforcement of federal law; are necessary to implement the state's decision to remove penalties for certain marijuana-related activities; do not immunize or shield the holder from federal prosecution; and, therefore, are not preempted. Moreover, it could be argued that a state license acts only as a means by which the state can impose controls on the production and distribution of marijuana under state law and to identify which individuals have been preapproved to engage in marijuana-related activities. This appears to be the approach taken by the United States Bankruptcy Court for the District of Colorado in an opinion focusing on whether a debtor, who leased space for the purposes of growing medicinal marijuana in compliance with state law, was engaged in an ongoing criminal activity.[116] In what is perhaps the only statement by a federal court relating to preemption of the Colorado and Washington laws, in *In re: Rent-Rite Super Kegs West LTD*, a bankruptcy court noted (in what was clearly dicta) that "conflict preemption is not an issue here. Colorado constitutional amendments for both medical marijuana, and the more recent amendment legalizing marijuana possession and usage generally, both make it clear that their provisions apply to state law only. Absent from either enactment is any effort to impede the enforcement of federal law."[117]

In addition, it has previously been argued that because the licensing and regulatory aspects of medical marijuana laws actually place additional *restrictions* on access to marijuana, those provisions are more consistent with the objectives of the CSA than the state decision to legalize marijuana production, distribution, possession.[118] By *limiting* marijuana and production and distribution, it could be argued that the envisioned Colorado and Washington regulatory and licensing provisions "further[] rather than obstruct[] the purposes of the CSA."[119] Under this reasoning, the Washington and Colorado regulatory and licensing aspects could be seen as supporting the federal government's objectives of "control[ing] the legitimate and illegitimate traffic in controlled substances," as opposed to creating an obstacle to that goal.

Taxation

In addition to regulating and licensing recreational marijuana use, both Colorado and Washington plan to impose a substantial excise tax on marijuana sales. In Colorado, the tax (which may not exceed 15% prior to January 1, 2017) is to be levied on sales of marijuana by cultivation facilities, product manufacturing facilities, or retail stores.[120] In Washington, a 25% tax is to be imposed at each transaction within the distribution chain, including sales from:

producer to processor; processor to retailer; and from retailer to consumer.[121] Although little precedent exists relating to state-imposed taxes on medical marijuana, there is evidence to suggest that these taxes would likely be considered permissible.

The Supreme Court has held that a state may "legitimately tax criminal activities."[122] Indeed, in *Department of Revenue of Montana v. Ranch*, the Court specifically suggested, in dicta, that it was within Montana's authority to tax the possession of marijuana.[123] The Montana law challenged in *Ranch* imposed a tax on the possession of illegal drugs. Although determining that the law's application to the petitioners violated the Double Jeopardy Clause of the Fifth Amendment by subjecting an individual to successive punishments for the same offense, the Court noted briefly that "Montana no doubt could collect its tax on the possession of Marijuana ... if it had not previously punished the taxpayer for the same offense."[124] The Court made clear that "as a general matter, the unlawfulness of an activity does not prevent its taxation."[125] In addition, many states already tax marijuana and other illegal or controlled substances. For example, 20 states require all possessors of marijuana to purchase "tax stamps."[126] Although some of these laws have raised questions relating to the Fifth Amendment's privilege against self-incrimination and double jeopardy clause, no court has found a state drug tax law to be preempted by federal law.

Moreover, if analyzing state marijuana taxes within the previously discussed preemption framework, it would appear difficult to argue that by imposing a tax on marijuana the state has authorized conduct prohibited under federal law or imposed an obstacle to the achievement of federal objectives. Taxes are generally imposed to either raise revenue, deter conduct, or both. Taxes on cigarettes for example, exist both to raise revenue and to deter smoking.127 The excise taxes envisioned by Colorado and Washington appear to be motivated by a desire to raise revenue to both pay for the regulatory and licensing controls on marijuana and to contribute to other budgetary needs, most notably health services and education. In addition, the Washington law states that the Liquor Control Board is authorized to make recommendations to adjust the tax levels "that would *further the goal of discouraging use* while undercutting illegal market prices."[128] The Colorado law does not explicitly reference any goal of deterring marijuana use, but it would appear that the envisioned tax may also have that effect. Thus, the state tax may more accurately be characterized as "interposing and economic impediment to the activity" as opposed to *authorizing* the activity.[129]

ARE THE WASHINGTON AND COLORADO LAWS PREEMPTED BY INTERNATIONAL LAW?

The United States is a party to various treaties that impose international obligations relating to the control of marijuana. These treaties generally seek to curb the use of controlled substances while carving out exceptions for "medicinal and scientific" uses.[130] The principle governing treaty in international drug control, which has been agreed to by more than 180 nations, is the Single Convention on Narcotic Drugs (Single Convention).[131] The Single Convention imposes restrictions on the manufacturing, distribution, and trade in narcotic drugs by establishing a multi- schedule classification structure that applies varying controls for each schedule. This framework later served as the blueprint for the CSA and other foreign drug control statutes.

"Cannabis" is listed as a Schedule I substance under the Single Convention and is therefore subject to the agreement's most restrictive controls.[132] For example, parties must "take such legislative and administrative measures as may be necessary ... to limit exclusively to medical and scientific purposes the production, manufacture, export, import, distribution of, trade in, use and possession of drugs"; limit the quantity of the drug manufactured and imported to "the quantity consumed ... for medical and scientific purposes"; and furnish the International Narcotics Control Board with information, estimates, and statistics related to the consumption and production of the drug.[133]

In addition to the Single Convention, the 1971 Convention on Psychotropic Substances requires that specific controls be placed by parties upon THC, the physiologically active chemical in marijuana,[134] while the 1988 United Nations Convention Against Illicit Traffic in Narcotic Drugs and Psychotropic Substances requires parties to establish criminal penalties for the possession, purchase, or cultivation of marijuana for nonmedicinal consumption, but only to the extent that such action is consistent with the "constitutional principles and basic concepts of [the country's] legal system."[135]

Both the U.S. Drug Enforcement Agency (DEA) and the U.S. Department of State have determined that in order to comply with these international obligations, it is necessary that marijuana remain on either Schedule I or Schedule II of the federal CSA.[136] The DEA, for example, has cited the nation's obligations under the Single Convention as the legal justification for denying rulemaking petitions requesting that the Attorney General exercise his authority under the CSA to remove marijuana entirely from control, or to transfer marijuana to Schedule III or lower.

The legalization measures enacted by Washington and Colorado would appear to be inconsistent with the obligations imposed upon the United States under existing international drug control treaties. However, existing jurisprudence suggests that a reviewing court may not view these treaty obligations, in and of themselves, as sufficient to preempt and invalidate the state laws.[137]

It is well established that treaties, like federal statutes, may preempt conflicting state laws. The Supremacy Clause expressly provides that in addition to federal law, "all treaties made ... under the authority of the United States, shall be the supreme law of the land."[138] Therefore, a state law is generally preempted to the same degree whether it is in conflict with a federal statute or an international treaty obligation. However, not all treaties are accorded "automatic" preemptive effect.[139] Only where a treaty "constitute[s] binding federal law," without the "aid of any [implementing] legislative provision," does it qualify as the "Supreme law of the land" for preemption purposes.[140] Such treaties are known as "self-executing" treaties—meaning an international agreement with "automatic domestic effect as federal law upon ratification."[141]

The Supreme Court recently clarified the distinction between the preemptive effect of self- executing and non-self-executing treaties in *Medellin v. Texas*.[142] *Medellin* involved an evaluation of whether a decision of the International Court of Justice (ICJ)—and a series of underlying international agreements that required compliance with ICJ decisions—constituted enforceable federal law with the authority to preempt Texas procedural court rules. In holding that the state court rules were not preempted, the court noted that it had "long recognized the distinction between treaties that automatically have effect as domestic law, and those that ... do not by themselves function as binding federal law."[143] Although the ICJ decision had clearly represented an "international obligation," it did not "of its own force constitute binding federal law that preempts state restrictions."[144]

Like the ICJ decision at issue in *Medellin*, neither the Single Convention nor the other international drug control treaties appear to be "self-executing." Each treaty requires the signatory nation to give legal effect to the goals of the treaty through domestic implementing legislation. The provisions of the treaties do not themselves establish binding domestic law. The United States, for example, implemented the obligations of these treaties through the CSA.[145] Because these treaties do not create binding law "of [their] own force," it would appear unlikely that a U.S. court would accord the treaties direct preemptive effect.[146] Indeed, in *County of San Diego*, the California court explicitly rejected treaty preemption arguments on the grounds that the Single convention is non-self-executing.[147] Thus it would appear unlikely that the Washington and Colorado laws would be found to be preempted by existing international obligations.[148]

POTENTIAL DOJ RESPONSES TO DETER MARIJUANA ACTIVITIES AND ENFORCE FEDERAL LAW

During a March 2013 Senate Judiciary Committee oversight hearing, Attorney General Eric Holder was asked by Senator Patrick Leahy about marijuana legalization in Colorado and Washington. General Holder replied that the Obama Administration is still in the process of reviewing the state marijuana laws and considering the appropriate federal response; he promised to announce a formal agency policy toward the marijuana legalization laws "relatively soon."[149] Absent such guidance, this report will highlight some potential options that the Department of Justice (DOJ) may have at its disposal in responding to the Washington and Colorado laws. The doctrine of prosecutorial discretion gives the DOJ great leeway in choosing whether, and to what extent, to bring criminal prosecutions for violations of the CSA within Colorado and Washington. In addition, the DOJ may utilize the CSA forfeiture provision to deter certain activities without actually engaging in criminal prosecutions. Finally, the DOJ may ask the federal judiciary to directly invalidate the state laws by filing a civil lawsuit.

Criminal Prosecutions

Criminal prosecutions are perhaps the DOJ's most potent tool for undercutting the Washington and Colorado laws. However, the DOJ is not required to zealously enforce every violation of the CSA. Indeed, pursuant to the doctrine of "prosecutorial discretion," federal law enforcement officials have "broad discretion" as to when, whom, and whether to prosecute for violations of the CSA.[150] Courts have recognized that the "decision to prosecute is particularly ill-suited to judicial review," as it involves the consideration of factors, such as the strength of evidence, deterrence value, and existing enforcement priorities, "not readily susceptible to the kind of analysis the courts are competent to undertake."[151] It would appear that the frequency with which the DOJ chooses to prosecute for violations of the CSA will likely have a substantial effect on the willingness of individuals to engage in state-approved marijuana activities in Washington and Colorado.

Through the exercise of prosecutorial discretion, the DOJ is free to develop a policy outlining what marijuana-related activities will receive the most attention from federal authorities. For example, in 2009 Deputy Attorney General David W. Ogden provided guidance to federal prosecutors in states that have authorized the use of medical marijuana.[152] Citing a desire to make "efficient and rational use of its limited investigative and prosecutorial resources," the memorandum stated that while the "prosecution of significant traffickers of illegal drugs, including marijuana ... continues to be a core priority," federal prosecutors "should not focus federal resources [] on individuals whose actions are in clear and unambiguous compliance with existing state laws providing for the medical use of marijuana."[153] The memorandum made clear, however, that "this guidance [does not] preclude investigation or prosecution, even where there is clear and unambiguous compliance with existing state law, in particular circumstances where investigation or prosecution otherwise serves important federal interests."[154] The DOJ released a subsequent memorandum two years later drawing a clear distinction between the potential prosecutions of individual patients who require marijuana in the course of medical treatment and "commercial" dispensaries.[155] After noting that several jurisdictions had recently "enacted legislation to authorize multiple large-scale, privately operated industrial marijuana cultivation centers," the DOJ stated that

> The Ogden memorandum was never intended to shield such activities from federal enforcement action and prosecution, even where those activities purport to comply with state law. Persons who are in the business of cultivating, selling or distributing marijuana, and those who knowingly facilitate such activities, are in violation of the [CSA] regardless of state law. Consistent with resource constraints and the discretion you may exercise in your district, such persons are subject to federal enforcement action, including potential prosecution.[156]

The DOJ may provide similar guidance to U.S. Attorneys within Washington and Colorado. The department could react strongly to the new laws, and encourage U.S. Attorneys to prosecute any violation of the CSA—including possession by individuals, distribution by marijuana retailers, and cultivation by marijuana producers. Although the DOJ may adopt this approach, as a practical matter, the federal government simply does not currently have the resources necessary to robustly enforce federal drug laws without the assistance of state authorities. Indeed, approximately 99% of drug offenses are prosecuted under state law by state authorities. Therefore, if a decision were made to increase the frequency of federal prosecutions in order to enforce federal law, new resources would likely be needed by the FBI, DEA, and the U.S. Attorneys. On the other end of the spectrum, the DOJ could simply defer to the state policy and halt prosecutions for violations of the CSA in Washington and Colorado, so long as the individual is in compliance with state law. Such an action may be fraught with long-term risks and pose a threat to federal supremacy by acknowledging that states are free to make policy decisions in direct conflict with those made at the federal level.

Perhaps the most likely approach, however, is one that reflects the DOJ's position on medical marijuana and adopts the middle ground between the robust enforcement of federal law and full deference to the state policies. Such an approach would likely focus prosecutions on those engaged in the large scale cultivation, distribution, or sale of marijuana, while overlooking individual possession of marijuana in compliance with state law. Although recognizing that the conduct remains a violation of federal law, the DOJ could make clear that prosecuting individuals for simple possession is not an agency priority. In conjunction with this approach, the DOJ may also warn marijuana producers, processors, and retailers about their potential to face asset forfeiture proceedings or criminal prosecution, in the hope that the facilities will voluntarily cease operation.

Forfeiture

Either in addition to, or in lieu of bringing criminal prosecutions, the DOJ may choose to rely more heavily on the civil forfeiture provisions of the CSA in order to disrupt the operation of marijuana dispensaries and production facilities. Forfeiture is a penalty associated with a particular crime in which property is confiscated or otherwise divested from the owner and forfeited to the government, in accordance with constitutionally required due process procedures.[157] Property forfeiture is used both to enforce criminal laws and to deter crime. Forfeitures are classified as civil or criminal depending on the nature of the judicial procedure which ends in confiscation. Civil forfeiture is ordinarily the product of a civil, *in rem* (against the property) proceeding in which the property is treated as the offender. No criminal charges are necessary against the owner because the guilt or innocence of the property owner is irrelevant; it is enough that the property was involved in, or otherwise connected to, an illegal activity (in which forfeiture is authorized). Criminal forfeiture proceedings, on the other hand, are *in personam* (against the person) actions, and confiscation is only possible upon the conviction of the owner of the property and only to the extent of the defendant's interest in the property.[158] Property that is subject to forfeiture includes both the direct and indirect proceeds of illegal activities as well as any property used, or intended to be used, to facilitate that crime.[159]

Section 511 of the CSA (21 U.S.C. §881) makes a wide array of property associated with violations of the CSA subject to seizure by the Attorney General and forfeiture to the United States. Property subject to the CSA's civil forfeiture provision includes any controlled substance that has been manufactured, distributed, dispensed, acquired, or possessed in violation of federal law, as well as any equipment, firearm, money, mode of transportation, or real property *used or intended to be used to facilitate a violation of the CSA*.[160] In order to seize the covered property, the government need only show that the property is subject to forfeiture by a preponderance of the evidence.[161] Once forfeited, the Attorney General may destroy the controlled substances seized, and sell the other property at public auction.[162] After expenses of the forfeiture proceeding are recouped, excess funds are forwarded to the DOJ Asset Forfeiture Fund.[163]

Forfeiture proceedings are generally less resource intensive than a criminal prosecution and have been used in the past against medical marijuana dispensaries.[164] In practice, the DOJ would be able to seize and liquidate property, both real and personal, associated with marijuana production distribution and retail sale facilities operating in Colorado and Washington without bringing any criminal action. As explained above, a civil asset forfeiture proceeding is a civil proceeding against the property in question. Although an interested party may object to the seizure, given that such facilities are in clear violation of federal law, so long as the property is indeed being used for marijuana-related activities, it would appear unlikely that many successful challenges to these actions could be waged.[165]

Civil Lawsuit

The broadest single action the DOJ could take to prevent the implementation of the Colorado and Washington laws would be to directly challenge the laws in federal court on the grounds that they are preempted by federal law.[166] Procedurally speaking, this lawsuit would look very much like the federal government's recent challenge of a controversial Arizona immigration law.[167] If the federal government chose to file such a claim, and a federal court were to reach the merits, the court would likely be forced to directly confront the preemption issues identified in the previous sections.

Additional Legal Consequences of Marijuana Use

Given the Obama Administration's informal statements and current approach to medical marijuana, it would appear unlikely that the DOJ is going to expend significant resources to investigate and prosecute individuals who merely possess and use less than one ounce of marijuana, in private, pursuant to Washington or Colorado law. However, even if the probability of becoming the subject of a federal criminal prosecution for a violation of the CSA appears remote, there does exist a number of other consequences under federal law that are triggered by the mere use of marijuana, even absent an arrest or conviction. Perhaps most prominent among these concerns is the possibility that marijuana users may lose their ability to purchase and possess a firearm, be barred from living in public housing, or find themselves subject to employment consequences in the workplace.

Under the Gun Control Act, it is unlawful to possess, ship, transport, receive, or dispose of any firearm or ammunition to any person "who is an unlawful user of or addicted to any controlled substance" as defined by the CSA.[168] Federal regulation defines an "unlawful user" or addict of a controlled substance as one who "has lost the power of self-control with reference to the controlled substance; and any person who is a current user of a controlled substance in a manner other than as prescribed by a licensed physician."[169] Furthermore, a person may be considered an unlawful user even if he is not using the substance at the precise time the person seeks to acquire a firearm or receives or possesses a firearm. However, after state laws regarding medical marijuana were enacted, the Bureau of Alcohol, Tobacco Firearms, and Explosives (ATF) issued an open notice stating that "any person who uses or is addicted to marijuana, regardless of whether his or her State has passed legislation authorizing marijuana use for medicinal purposes, is an unlawful user of or addicted to a controlled substance, and is prohibited by Federal law from possessing firearms or ammunition."[170] These individuals are to answer "yes" when asked on the firearms transfer form if they are unlawful users of a controlled substance. With the legalization of marijuana for recreational purposes in Colorado and Washington, it seems likely the ATF will take the same approach and consider a recreational user of marijuana to be a prohibited possessor of firearms regardless of whether the use is lawful under state provisions.

In addition to potentially losing the ability to purchase and possess a firearm, federal law also establishes that "illegal drug users" are ineligible for federally assisted housing.[171] 42 U.S.C. §§13661 and 13662 require public housing agencies and owners of federally assisted housing to establish standards that would allow the agency or owner to prohibit admission to, or terminate the tenancy or assistance of, any applicant or tenant. An agency or an owner can take these actions if a determination is made, pursuant to the standards established, that an individual is "illegally using a controlled substance," or if there is reasonable cause to believe that an individual has a "pattern of illegal use" of a controlled substance that could "interfere with the health, safety, or right to a peaceful enjoyment of the premises by other residents."[172] Under federal law, marijuana remains a controlled substance, thus, it would appear that any individual who the housing authority reasonably believes is using marijuana could be denied access to, or evicted from, federally assisted housing. With respect to medical marijuana, the Department of Housing and Urban Development previously concluded that public housing agencies or owners "must deny *admission*" to applicants who are using medical marijuana, but "have statutorily- authorized discretion with respect to evicting or refraining from evicting *current residents* on account of their use of medical marijuana."[173]

Some employers may face the loss of federal funding or could be subject to administrative fines if they do not maintain and enforce policies aimed at achieving a drug-free, safe workplace. The federal Drug-Free Workplace Act of 1988 (DFWA)[174] imposes a drug-free workplace requirement on any entity that receives federal contracts with a value of more than $100,000 or that receives any federal grant.[175] DFWA requires these entities to make ongoing, good faith efforts to comply with the drug-free workplace requirement in order to qualify, and remain eligible, for federal funds.[176] Employees who work for federal contractors and grantees could potentially be subject to employer discipline or even termination if they use marijuana while on the job or show up for work under the influence of marijuana, even if the marijuana use is permitted by state law, as such usage may create risks to others' safety.[177] (Similarly, the Drug-Free Schools and Communities Act Amendment of 1989[178] renders any institution of higher education ineligible for federal funding if it fails to establish and implement a program to prevent the abuse of illicit drugs by students and employees on campus grounds.) In addition, employers under the jurisdiction of the Occupational Safety and Health Administration have a general duty to provide to their employees a safe workplace under the Occupational Safety and Health Act.[179] An employee who uses marijuana at work may be considered a workplace hazard if he or she poses a danger to other workers; employers thus risk administrative fines if they do not enforce policies that seek to avoid such a hazard.

Congressional Response

Several bills concerning marijuana have been introduced that reflect different approaches in response to the state legalization initiatives.

H.R. 499, Ending Federal Marijuana Prohibition Act of 2013. This bill would direct the Attorney General to issue a final order, within 60 days of the bill's enactment, that entirely removes marijuana from any CSA schedule.[180] In addition, the bill would amend the CSA by adding a new Section 103 that declares that no provision of the CSA shall apply to marijuana, with the following new exception: shipping or transporting marijuana from anywhere outside a jurisdiction of the United States into such a jurisdiction where marijuana use, possession, or sale is prohibited.[181] The bill would make conforming amendments to the CSA as well as other sections of the *U.S. Code* to expressly remove the word "marijuana" or "marihuana" from various penalty, enforcement, and definition provisions.[182] The bill also would amend the Federal Alcohol Administration Act[183] to create a new section entitled "Unlawful Businesses Without Marijuana Permit."[184] This section would make it unlawful to engage in importing, shipping, or selling marijuana in interstate or foreign commerce, or cultivating, producing, manufacturing, packaging, or warehousing marijuana, without a permit issued by the Secretary of the Treasury. The criminal fine for persons engaging in such activity without a permit would be not more than $1,000, although the Secretary would be allowed to collect a payment from the violator of up to $500 in lieu of referring the violation to the Attorney General for prosecution. The Secretary would have to follow specific eligibility criteria set forth in the bill in selecting applicants for a marijuana business permit and the Secretary would also be required to establish a reasonable permit fee to cover the cost of implementing and overseeing all aspects of federal regulation of marijuana. Finally, the bill would grant the Food and Drug Administration the same authorities with respect to marijuana as it has with respect to alcohol,[185] and would transfer all current functions of the DEA Administrator relating to marijuana enforcement to the Director of the Bureau of Alcohol, Tobacco, Firearms and Explosives.[186]

H.R. 501, Marijuana Tax Equity Act of 2013. This bill would amend the Internal Revenue Code to impose an excise tax on the sale of marijuana by the producer or importer of the drug, equivalent to 50 percent of the price for which it was sold.[187] In addition, the bill would require anyone engaged in a "marijuana enterprise"[188] to pay an occupational tax in the amount of $1,000 per year (for producers, importers, or manufacturers of marijuana), or $500 per year (for distributors, retailers, or anyone who transports, stores, or displays marijuana products).[189] The bill would require all individuals, prior to commencing business as a marijuana enterprise, to obtain a permit from the Secretary of the Treasury.[190] Finally, the bill would impose civil and criminal penalties for violation of the duty to pay the new taxes regarding marijuana as well as engaging in business as a marijuana enterprise without obtaining the requisite permit.[191]

H.R. 689, *States' Medical Marijuana Patient Protection Act.* This bill would direct the Secretary of Health and Human Services, in cooperation with the National Academy of Sciences' Institute of Medicine, to submit to the DEA Administrator a recommendation on the scheduling of marijuana within the CSA, although the bill precludes the Secretary from selecting either Schedule I or II.[192] The Secretary would be required to issue such recommendation within 180 days of the enactment of the bill, and the DEA administrator would need to issue a proposed rulemaking for the rescheduling of marijuana in accordance with the recommendation within a year of enactment of the bill.[193] The legislation declares that no provision of the CSA, nor any provision of the Federal Food, Drug, and Cosmetic Act,[194] shall prohibit or otherwise restrict in a state where the medical use of marijuana is lawful under state law, the production, prescription, transportation, distribution, possession, or use of marijuana for medical use.[195] Finally, the bill would require the Attorney General, within 180 days of the bill's enactment, to transfer control over access to marijuana for research purposes (currently the responsibility of the National Institute on Drug Abuse, a component of the National Institutes of Health, U.S. Department of Health and Human Services) to an Executive Branch entity "that is not focused on researching the addictive properties of substances."[196] The bill would require such entity to "take appropriate actions to ensure that an adequate supply of marijuana is available for therapeutic and medicinal research."[197]

H.R. 710, Truth in Trials Act. This bill would amend the federal criminal code (Title 18 of the *U.S. Code*) to provide an affirmative defense for conduct regarding the medical use of marijuana in a prosecution or proceeding for any marijuana-related offense under any federal law. Individuals asserting such defense must establish, by a preponderance of the evidence, that their marijuana-related activities were conducted in compliance with state law regarding medical use of marijuana.[198] The bill would require that any property seized by the government in connection with such prosecution or proceeding be returned to the owner within 10 days of the court finding that the owner has established a valid affirmative defense.[199] Finally, the bill would permit a court to hold liable for the marijuana-related offense a defendant who has engaged primarily, but not exclusively, in medical marijuana activities, only with respect to the amount of marijuana that was used for nonmedical purposes.[200]

H.R. 784, States' Medical Marijuana Property Rights Protection Act. This bill would amend the civil forfeiture provisions of the CSA[201] to provide that no real property may be subject to civil forfeiture to the United States due to medical marijuana-related activities that are performed in compliance with state law.[202]

H.R. 964, *Respect States' and Citizens' Rights Act of 2013.* This bill would amend the CSA's preemption provision, Section 708 (codified at 21 U.S.C. §903), to provide a specific rule of construction pertaining to state marijuana laws: that no provision of the CSA shall be construed as—(1) indicating an intent on the part of Congress to occupy the field in which that provision operates, including criminal penalties, to the exclusion of state law regarding marijuana, or (2) preempting any such state law.[203]

End Notes

[1] *New State Ice Co. v. Liebmann*, 285 U. S. 262, 311 (1932) (Brandeis, J., dissenting).

[2] U.S. CONST., Art. VI, cl. 2.

[3] For a discussion of state medical marijuana laws, *see* CRS Report R42398, *Medical Marijuana: The Supremacy Clause, Federalism, and the Interplay Between State and Federal Laws*, by Todd Garvey.

[4] It is important to distinguish between two common terms that have been used to describe state marijuana laws: legalization and decriminalization. For purposes of this report, a state "legalizes" conduct when an individual who engages in that conduct is not subject to any state penalty. A state decriminalizes conduct when criminal penalties are removed, but civil penalties remain. This report characterizes the Washington and Colorado laws as legalization initiatives because each state has removed all state-imposed penalties for qualified marijuana activities. The legalization initiatives are to be distinguished from state marijuana decriminalization measures, like that of Massachusetts, which remove criminal penalties for possession of small amounts of marijuana, but retain civil penalties. It is important to note, however, that the term legalization is itself misleading, as a state cannot fully "legalize" conduct that constitutes a crime under federal law.

[5] Reports suggest that the number of jurisdictions that have legalized either medicinal or recreational marijuana will likely continue to grow. *See, e.g.*, Tim Dickinson, *The Next Seven States To Legalize Pot*, ROLLING STONE, December 18, 2012.

[6] 21 U.S.C. §841(b); 21 U.S.C. §844(b).

[7] *See, e.g.*, United States v. Stacy, 734 F. Supp. 2d 1074, 1079 (S.D. Cal. 2010) ("[T]he fact that an individual may not be prosecuted under [state] law does not provide him or her with immunity under federal law."); United States v. Rosenthal, 454 F.3d 943 (9th Cir. 2006) (holding that state medical marijuana law could not act as a shield to federal prosecution).

[8] *See* Statement From U.S. Attorney's Office on Initiative 502, DOJ Press Release, December 5, 2012, *available at* http://www.justice.gov/usao/waw/press/2012/December/Statement.html; *Devin Dwyer, Marijuana Not High Obama Priority*, ABC NEWS, December 14, 2012, *available at* http://abcnews.go.com/Politics/OTUS/president-obama- marijuana-users-high-priority-drug-war/story?id=17946783#.UVmtVVE4gpV.

[9] *See* Josh Gerstein, *Holder: Feds to Set Pot Legalization Response "Relatively Soon,"* POLITICO, February 26, 2013, *at* http://www.politico.com/blogs/under-the-radar/2013/02/holder-feds-to-set-pot-legalization-response-relatively- 157895.html.

[10] Washington Initiative 502 at §20, amending RCW 69.50.4013 and 2003 c 53 s 334, *available at* http://sos.wa.gov/_assets/elections/initiatives/i502.pdf.

[11] *Id.* at §15.

[12] *Id.* at §21.

[13] *Id.* at §4.

[14] *Id.*

[15] *Id.* at §10.

[16] *Id.* §9-10.

[17] *Id.* at §27.

[18] *Id.* at §26.

[19] *Id.* §31.

[20] Colorado Amendment 64, Amending Colo. Const. Art. XVIII §16(3), *available at* http://www.colorado.gov/cs/Satellite?blobcol=urldata&blobheader=application/pdf&blobkey=id&blobtable=MungoBlobs&blobwhere= 1251822971738&ssbinary=true.

[21] *Id.*

[22] *Id.*

[23] *Id.* at §16(4).

[24] The licensing and regulatory systems envisioned by both Colorado and Washington are modeled on similar state alcohol distribution schemes found across the country.
[25] Colorado Amendment 64, at §16(5).
[26] *Id.*
[27] *Id.* at §16(5)(d).
[28] *Id.* at §16(6). It should be noted that a state license is required to sell marijuana in either state.
[29] Task Force Report on the Implementation of Amendment 64, March 13, 2013 at 9. Available at http://www.colorado.gov/cms/forms/dor-tax/A64TaskForceFinalReport.pdf.
[30] *Id.* at 16-19.
[31] *Id.* at 28-31.
[32] *Id.* at 33.
[33] *Id.* at 49-51.
[34] 21 U.S.C. §§801 et seq. In *Gonzales v. Raich,* the U.S. Supreme Court ruled that Congress had the constitutional authority under the Commerce Clause to prohibit the wholly intrastate cultivation or possession of marijuana for medical purposes, despite state laws that permit such activity. 545 U.S. 1 (2005); for more information about this decision, *see* CRS Report RL32844, *The Power to Regulate Commerce: Limits on Congressional Power*, by Kenneth R. Thomas.
[35] P.L. 91-513, 84 Stat. 1236 (1970).
[36] 21 U.S.C. §§811-812.
[37] The Attorney General delegated his authority under the CSA to the DEA Administrator pursuant to 21 U.S.C. §871(a); 28 C.F.R. §0.100(b).
[38] For more information about these requirements, *see* CRS Report RL34635, *The Controlled Substances Act: Regulatory Requirements*, by Brian T. Yeh.
[39] For a detailed description of the CSA's civil and criminal provisions, *see* CRS Report RL30722, *Drug Offenses: Maximum Fines and Terms of Imprisonment for Violation of the Federal Controlled Substances Act and Related Laws*, by Brian T. Yeh.
[40] 21 U.S.C. §812(b)(1).
[41] 21 U.S.C. §823(f).
[42] *See* 21 C.F.R. §1306.03 (persons entitled to issue prescriptions).
[43] 21 C.F.R. §1306.04; United States v. Moore, 4223 U.S. 122 (1975).
[44] The procedures for these actions are found at 21 U.S.C. §811.
[45] 21 U.S.C. §811(a).
[46] 21 U.S.C. §812(c).
[47] Very narrow exceptions to the federal prohibition do exist. For example, one may legally use marijuana if participating in an FDA approved study or participate in the Compassionate Investigational New Drug program.
[48] 21 U.S.C. §844(a).
[49] 21 U.S.C. §844(a).
[50] 21 U.S.C. §841(b).
[51] U.S. CONST., Art. VI, cl. 2.
[52] See discussion of preemptive effect of treaties *infra*.
[53] Northern States Power Co. v. Minnesota, 447 F.2d 1143, 1145 (8th Cir. 1971).
[54] *See, e.g.*, Wickard v. Filburn, 317 U.S. 111, 124 (1942)("[N]o form of state activity can constitutionally thwart the regulatory power granted by the commerce clause to Congress").
[55] Hines v. Davidowitz, 312 U.S. 52, 67 (1941); *See also*, English v. General Elec. Co., 496 U.S. 72, 79 (1990) ("By referring to these three categories, we should not be taken to mean that they are rigidly distinct.").
[56] *See, e.g.*, English v. General Elec. Co., 496 U.S. 72, 79 (1990).
[57] There is, however, a presumption against federal preemption when it comes to the exercise of "historic police powers of the States." Rice v. Santa Fe Elevator Corp., 331 U.S. 218, 230 (1947). Where Congress legislates within is area of traditional state control, courts generally

imply preemption only where it is the "clear and manifest purpose of Congress." *Id.* State laws defining criminal conduct and regulating drugs are generally accorded this presumption.

[58] *Santa Fe Elevator Corp.*, 331 U.S. at 230 (1947).

[59] *See*, Gade v. National Solid Waste Management Assn., 505 U.S. 88, 98 (1992)(emphasis added).

[60] Skull Valley Band of Goshute Indians v. Nielson, 376 F.3d 1223, 1240 (10th Cir. 2004) (*citing* Wardair Canada, Inc. v. Florida Dep't of Revenue 477 U.S. 1 (1986)).

[61] A number of courts have held that the CSA does not contain an "express preemption" provision. *See, e.g.,* Ter Beek v. City of Wyoming, 2012 Mich. App. LEXIS 1510 (July 31, 2012) (stating that "express preemption is inapplicable because there is no express preemption provision in the CSA"). It is not entirely clear why 21 U.S.C. §903 would not constitute such a provision. Although not imperative to the preemption analysis, it would seem that an express preemption provision includes any provision in which Congress expressly articulates the preemptive effect of a federal statute. English v. General Elec. Co., 496 U.S. 72, 79 (1990) (observing that express preemption exists when Congress "define[s] explicitly the extent to which its enactments pre-empt state law."). 21 U.S.C. §903 would appear to meet that definition as it describes what state laws Congress did, and did not, intend to be preempted.

[62] 21 U.S.C. §903 (emphasis added).

[63] Gonzales v. Oregon, 546 U.S. 243, 251 (2006).

[64] *See, e.g.*, Emerald Steel Fabricators, Inc., v. Bureau of Labor and Industries, 348 Ore. 159 (2010); Qualified Patients Assoc. v. City of Anaheim, 187 Cal. App. 4th 734 (2010); Ter Beek v. City of Wyoming, 2012 Mich. App. LEXIS 1510 (July 31, 2012).

[65] *See, e.g.,* County of San Diego v. San Diego NORML, 165 Cal. App. 4th 798 (2008)(holding that a state law conflicts with the CSA only where it is impossible to comply with both the state and federal law.).

[66] Wyeth v. Levine, 555 U.S. 555 (2009).

[67] *Id.* at 1195-96.

[68] The impossibility prong of the conflict preemption test has been characterized as "vanishingly narrow. " Caleb Nelson, *Preemption,* 86 VA. L. REV. 225, 228 (2000).

[69] *See* Barnett Bank v. Nelson, 517 U.S. 25 (1996).

[70] *See, e.g., Emerald Steel*, 348 Ore. at 175 ("[A] person can comply with both laws by refraining from any use of marijuana, in much the same way that a national bank could comply with state and federal law in *Barnett Bank* by simply refraining from selling insurance.").

[71] One provision of the Washington law may be construed as "requiring" an individual to violate federal law. Under §11 of the Initiative, "every licensed marijuana producer and processor must submit representative samples of marijuana ... produced or processed by the licensee to an independent, third party testing laboratory ..." Washington Initiative 502 §11. In *Pack v. City of Long Beach,* 199 Cal. app. 4th 1070, 1090-91 (2011) a California court held that a city ordinance that required marijuana collectives to submit samples of analysis appeared "to *require* that certain individuals violate the federal CSA."

[72] Although the Supreme Court has issued two decisions relating to the CSA's marijuana provisions, neither case discussed the preemption question. *See* Gonzales v. Raich, 545 U.S. 1 (2005)(holding that the CSA's prohibition on the local cultivation and use of marijuana was within Congress's authority); United States v. Oakland Cannabis Buyers' Cooperative, 532 U.S. 483 (2001)(holding that there is no medical necessity exception to the CSA).

[73] The Oregon Supreme Court appears to be the only state Supreme Court to directly consider the extent to which the CSA preempts state marijuana laws. With specific importance to the immediate analysis, it does not appear that any state court in Colorado or Washington has addressed the preemption issue.

[74] Wyeth v. Levine, 555 U.S. 555, 565 (2009).

[75] *Id.*

[76] Gonzales v Raich, 545 U.S. 1, 12 (2005). Moreover, in a case addressing whether the CSA prohibited physician assisted suicide, the court appears to have characterized the CSA "as a statute combating *recreational* drug abuse ..." It is clear, however, that with respect to marijuana, the CSA prohibits both recreational and medical uses.

[77] *Wyeth*, 555 U.S. at 565.

[78] Rice v. Santa Fe Elevator Corp., 331 U.S. 218 (1947). In these areas, a more "significant" conflict may be required before a state law constitutes an obstacle to the achievement of the federal goal. County of San Diego v. San Diego NORML, 165 Cal. App. 4th 798 (2008) (*citing* Boyle v. United Technologies Corp., 487 U.S. 500, 507 (1988)).

[79] Both state laws legalize only the possession of one ounce or less by individuals 21 years of age or older.

[80] As opposed to the federal government, which is one of limited and enumerated power, the states have retained "inherent police power," Newberry v. United States, 256 U.S. 232 (1921). This includes the power to legislate for the "health, safety, and morals" of the citizenry. Barnes v. Glen Theatre, Inc., 501 U.S. 560, 569 (1991).

[81] See, Printz v. United States, 521 U.S. 898 (1997); New York v. United States, 505 U.S. 144 (1992). In *Reno v. Condon*, the Supreme Court held that a federal law does not "commandeer" state resources so long as it "does not require the States in their sovereign capacities to regulate their own citizens," but rather regulates state activities directly. 528 U.S. 141, 151 (2000). See also, Gonzales v. Oregon, 546 U.S. 243, 270 (2006) ("the structure and limitations of federalism ... allow the States great latitude under their police powers to legislate as to the protection of the lives, limbs, health, comfort, and quiet of all persons.")(citations omitted).

[82] See, e.g., U.S. v. Lanza, 260 U.S. 377, 382 (1922)("We have here two sovereigns, deriving power from different sources, capable of dealing with the same subject matter within the same territory ... Each government in determining what shall be an offense against its peace and dignity is exercising its own sovereignty, not that of the other.").

[83] For a broader discussion of the principles of federalism embodied within the Tenth Amendment, *see* CRS Report RL30315, *Federalism, State Sovereignty, and the Constitution: Basis and Limits of Congressional Power*, by Kenneth R. Thomas. For a specific discussion of the Tenth Amendment's application to state and federal marijuana laws, *see* CRS Report R42398, *Medical Marijuana: The Supremacy Clause, Federalism, and the Interplay Between State and Federal Laws*, by Todd Garvey.

[84] Qualified Patients Assoc. v. City of Anaheim, 187 Cal. App. 4th 734 (2010) (*citing* Conant v. Walters, 309 F.3d 629, 646 (9th Cir. 2002) (Kozinski, J., concurring)

[85] *See*, Wyeth v. Levine, 555 U.S. 555 (2009); Barnett Bank v. Nelson, 517 U.S. 25 (1996).

[86] *Barnett Bank*, 517 U.S. at 31 (holding that a federal statute that permitted national banks to sell insurance and a state statute that prohibited banks from selling insurance did not "impose directly conflicting duties").

[87] Crosby v. National Foreign Trade Council, 530 U.S. 363, 373-74 (2000).

[88] *See, e.g.*, United States v. Oakland Cannabis Buyers' Cooperative, 532 U.S. 483 (2001)(holding that there is no medical necessity defense under the CSA, even where state law recognizes such a defense.); United States v. Rosenthal, 454 F.3d 943 (9th Cir. 2006) (holding that state medical marijuana law could not act as a shield to federal prosecution.); United States v. Stacy, 734 F. Supp. 2d 1074, 1079 (S.D. Cal. 2010) ("[T[he fact that an individual may not be prosecuted under [state] law does not provide him or her with immunity under federal law."); United States v. Lynch, 2010 U.S. Dist. LEXIS 53011(C.D. Cal. 2010).

[89] This is especially true within the marijuana context. See Ter Beek v. City of Wyoming, 2012 Mich. App. LEXIS 1510 (July 31, 2012) ("99 out of every 100 marijuana-based arrests in the United States are made under state law.").

[90] Although state medical marijuana exemptions have typically not been found to create an unacceptable obstacle to federal law, an argument could be forwarded that recreational

legalization measures, such as those in Colorado and Washington that permit marijuana use on a larger scale, could represent a more substantial barrier to the accomplishment of federal objectives. As a practical matter, even if a court were to adopt this reasoning and strike down the legalization provisions, neither the federal government nor a court can compel a state to make marijuana possession a criminal offense under state law. The potentially bizarre result may be that if prohibited from enacting an express provision of state law ensuring that "it shall not be unlawful to possess one ounce of marijuana," a state could simply choose to repeal all criminal provisions that apply to the possession of marijuana. The result as to the legality of marijuana possession under state criminal law would appear to be substantially the same whether the state affirmatively permits, or fails to proscribe certain conduct.

[91] City of Garden Grove v. Superior Ct. of Orange County, 157 Cal. App. 4th 355 (2007) (*citing Gonzales v. Raich*, 545 U.S. 1, 42 (2005) (O'Connor, J., dissenting).

[92] 467 U.S. 461 (1984).

[93] *Id.* at 477 ("The Michigan Act, however, empowers producers' associations to do precisely what the federal Act forbids them to do.").

[94] Emerald Steel Fabricators, Inc., v. Bureau of Labor and Industries, 348 Ore. 159, 230 P.3d 518 (2010).

[95] *Id.* at 525. The challenge to the law arose in the context of an employment discrimination claim in which an employee, who had obtained an identification card due to a medical condition, was allegedly discharged for admitting that he used marijuana. Oregon law requires that employers "make reasonable accommodations" for an employee's disability as long as such an accommodation does not impose an undue hardship upon the employer. However, the law is to be interpreted consistently with the federal Americans with Disabilities Act, which does not afford protections for employees "currently engaged in the illegal use of drugs."

[96] *Id.* at 526 n.12 ("The only issue that employer's preemption argument raises is whether federal law preempts ORS 475.306(1) to the extent that it authorizes the use of medical marijuana. In holding that federal law does preempt that subsection, we do not hold that federal law preempts the other sections of the Oregon Medical Marijuana Act that exempt medical marijuana use from criminal liability.")

[97] The court specifically noted that "the validity of the exemptions and the validity of the authorization turn on different constitutional principles." *Id.* at 530 Although Congress may "lack authority to require states to criminalize conduct that the states choose to leave unregulated ... [b]y contrast, there is no dispute that Congress has the authority under the Supremacy Clause to preempt state laws that affirmatively authorize the use of medical marijuana." *Id.*

[98] *Id.* at 529-30.

[99] *Id.* In a subsequent case evaluating whether the Oregon concealed handgun licensing statute was preempted by the Federal Gun Control Act, the Oregon Supreme Court arguably confined the authorization/exemption distinction, warning that "*Emerald Steel* should not be construed as announcing a stand-alone rule that any state law that can be viewed as "affirmatively authorizing" what federal law prohibits is preempted. Rather, it reflects this court's attempt to apply the federal rule and the logic of the most relevant federal cases to the particular preemption problem that was before it. And particularly where, as here, the issue of *whether* the statute contains an affirmative authorization is not straightforward, the analysis in *Emerald Steel* cannot operate as a simple stand-in for the more general federal rule." Willis v. Winters, 350 Or. 299, 253 P.3d 1058 (2011).

[100] 165 Cal. App. 4th 798 (2008), review denied 2008 Cal. LEXIS 12220 (Cal. 2008); 187 Cal. App. 4th 734 (2010).

[101] Notably, after considering the previously discussed "impossibility" and "obstacle" prongs of conflict preemption, the court in *County of San Diego*, concluded that the language of the CSA suggested that Congress "did not intend to supplant all laws posing some conceivable

obstacle to the purposes of the CSA." Thus, the court rejected the application of "obstacle" preemption under the CSA and held that a state law should only be preempted if it were impossible to simultaneously comply with both state and federal law. However, the court then went on to apply both the impossibility and the obstacle prong of the preemption analysis.

102 *Id.* at 825. The Court of Appeals of Michigan appears to have also adopted a similar line of reasoning, holding that the Michigan medical marijuana law "is not preempted by the CSA because it only grants immunity from state prosecution and, therefore, does not stand as an obstacle to the accomplishment and execution of the full purposes and objectives of Congress." Ter Beek v. City of Wyoming, 2012 Mich. App. LEXIS 1510 (July 31, 2012).

103 *Id.* at 827. The court also noted that "[a]lthough California's decision to enact statutory exemptions from state criminal prosecution for such persons arguably undermines the goals or is inconsistent with the CSA—a question we do not decide here—any alleged 'obstacle' to the federal goals is presented by those California statutes that create the exemptions, not by the statutes providing a system for rapidly identifying exempt individuals.").

104 530 U.S. 363 (2000).

105 187 Cal. App. 4th 734, 761-63 (2010).

106 *Id.* at 761.

107 199 Cal. App. 4th 1070, 1076 (2011) (appeal dismissed 283 P.3d 1159 (2012) ("In this case, we are concerned with a city ordinance which *goes beyond simple decriminalization*.") (emphasis in original).

108 As with previous cases, the court first found that "[s]ince a person can comply with both the federal CSA and the City ordinance by simply not being involved in the cultivation or possession of medical marijuana at all, there is no conflict [impossibility] preemption." *Id.* at 1090.

109 *Id.* at 1092-93.

110 *Id.* at 1093.

111 *Id.*

112 *Id.* at 1093.

113 Both initiatives require licensing of marijuana producers, processers, and sellers, and empower state agencies to promulgate broad rules and regulations to implement a regulatory and licensing scheme.

114 A reviewing court may also focus on the scope of the Colorado and Washington initiatives. In *County of San Diego* and *Qualified Patients*—cases in which the courts took an arguably less restrictive view of what constitutes an obstacle to federal objectives sufficient to trigger preemption—the court noted that the state medical marijuana laws in question related more to state medical practices than to the regulation of controlled substances. In both cases, the court asserted that the purpose of the CSA was to "combat recreational drug use, not to regulate a state's medical practices." *Qualified Patients*, 187 Cal. App. 4th at 760 (*citing County of San Diego,* 165 Cal. App. 4th at 826-27. The laws enacted in Colorado and Washington, which legalize, regulate, and license marijuana activities wholly unrelated to any medicinal purpose, cannot be characterized as a regulation of state medical practices. The reasoning applied by a California appellate court in *Garden City v. Superior Court of Orange County* may also support this concern. 157 Cal App. 4th 355 (2007). In *Garden City*, a California court held that a provision of the California medical marijuana law requiring that marijuana seized by local police be returned to qualified patients was not preempted by the CSA. The court noted that it was "unreasonable to believe" that returning seized marijuana would significantly "hinder the federal government's enforcement efforts" as "this subset of medical marijuana users is too small to make a measurable impact on the war on drugs." *Id.* at 384. If the California court found the "meager" numbers of individuals who would qualify for the return of seized marijuana to be noteworthy, it is possible that a court could alternatively be swayed by the much larger number of users that would qualify under the Colorado and Washington initiatives. Although it is impossible to identify the

impact the Colorado and Washington laws will have on marijuana use, a reviewing court could find that the scope of the initiatives present a "meaningful threat to the federal drug enforcement effort." *Id.*

[115] For a discussion of limitations on the federal government's ability to preempt state medical marijuana laws see, Robert a. Mikos, *Medical Marijuana and the States' Overlooked Power to Legalize Federal Crime*, 62 Vand. L. Rev. 1421 (2009).

[116] In re: Rent-Rite Super Kegs West Ltd., 484 B.R. 799 (Dec 19, 2012). Whether the debtor was engaged in criminal activity was an issue in the case because "a federal court cannot be asked to enforce the protections of the Bankruptcy Code in aid of a Debtor whose activities constitute a continuing federal crime." *Id.* at 805.

[117] *Id.* at 805 ("The fact that there is a difference in legislative philosophy creates no conflict that requires an analysis of federal preemption under the Supremacy Clause."). Part of the confusion over the proper application of obstacle preemption to state marijuana laws may stem from an apparent disagreement over the nature of the obstacle that is required to trigger preemption. As previously noted, the Supreme Court has held that a state law is preempted when it "stands as an obstacle *to the accomplishment and execution of the full purposes and objectives of Congress*." Most courts that have rejected preemption challenges to state medical marijuana laws have interpreted "the full purposes and objectives of Congress" in relation to the federal government's ability to enforce federal law. As such, these courts have generally held that because the state law does not create a shield or otherwise immunize state residents from federal criminal prosecutions, the law does not constitute an obstacle to "the enforcement of federal law." To the contrary, the Oregon Supreme Court reasoned that the fact that the state law in no way inhibited federal prosecutions did not mean that the law did not otherwise create an obstacle to the Congress's chief objective in enacting the CSA; that of curtailing drug use.

[118] See, Brief of Amici Curiae Professors of Constitutional and Criminal Law, Pack v. City of Long Beach, 199 Cal. App. 4th 1070 (2011) at 12-18. "Given that the Tenth Amendment permits California to decriminalize all medical marijuana activities, it defies reason to suggest that Congress intended to preempt localities from limiting the production, limiting the proliferation, and reducing the potential abuse of marijuana—all of which would serve to narrow the scope of a state policy that differs from federal policy." *Id.* at 16.

[119] *Id.*

[120] Washington Initiative 502 §27.

[121] Colorado Amendment 64, Amending Colo. Const. Art. XVIII §16(5)(d).

[122] Department of Revenue of Montana v. Ranch, 511 U.S. 767, 775 n.13 (1994) (*citing* Marchetti v. United States, 390 U.S. 39, 44 (1968)).

[123] 511 U.S. 767 (1994).

[124] *Id.* at 778.

[125] *Id.* at 788.

[126] See State Tax Stamp Data, available at http://norml.org/legal/tax-stamps. See also Robert A. Mikos, *State Taxation of Marijuana Distribution and Other Federal Crimes*, 2010 U. Chi. Legal F. 223 (2010).

[127] See, Nat'l Fed'n of Indep. Bus. v. Sebelius, 132 S. Ct. 2566, 2596 (U.S. 2012)

[128] Washington Initiative 502 §27.

[129] *Sebelius*, 132 S. Ct. at 2596 (U.S. 2012) ("To some extent it interposes an economic impediment to the activity taxed as compared with others not taxed.").

[130] See e.g., Single Convention on Narcotic Drugs art. 4, March 30, 1961, 18 U.S.T. 1407 ("The Parties shall take such legislative and administrative measures as may be necessary ... to limit exclusively to medical and scientific purposes the production, manufacture, export, import, distribution of, trade in, use and possession of drugs.").

[131] Single Convention on Narcotic Drugs, March 30, 1961, 18 U.S.T. 1407. The Single Convention was amended by the 1972 Protocol Amending the Single Convention on Narcotic Drugs.

[132] *Id.* at art. 2.

[133] *Id.* at art. 2,4, 21,28.

[134] Convention on Psychotropic Substances, February 21, 1971, 32 U.S.T. 543. The Convention directs parties to "prohibit all use except for scientific and very limited medical purposes by duly authorized persons, in medical or scientific establishments which are directly under the control of their Governments or specifically approved by them ..."

[135] December 20, 1988, S. Treaty Doc. No. 101-4 (1989).

[136] See 40 Fed. Reg. 44167, 44168 (September 25, 1975) (statement of the Acting Administrator of the DEA) ("The control mechanisms of the Act for Schedule I or Schedule II are sufficient to meet the obligations of the Single Convention as to the flowering or fruiting tops, seeds, and leaves when they accompany such tops, and resin.... The United States Department of State interprets the Single Convention to require U.S. control of the flowering or fruiting tops of the cannabis plant and cannabis resin in Schedule I or Schedule II of the Act."); *see also* Nat'l Org. for the Reform of Marijuana Laws v. Drug Enforcement Agency, 559 F.2d 735, 751 (D.C. Cir. 1977) (holding that, consistent with the Single Convention, "the United States could decline to restrict cannabis and cannabis resin to research purposes and could reschedule the drugs to CSA Schedule II.").

[137] For a discussion of the interplay between international agreements and U.S. law, see CRS Report RL32528, *International Law and Agreements: Their Effect Upon U.S. Law*, by Michael John Garcia. In addition, an international agreement that *required* states to enact certain marijuana controls may raise concerns under the 10th Amendment. Although the Supreme Court has recognized that Congress may enact legislation to implement U.S. treaty obligations that would otherwise infringe upon a state's traditional rights under the Tenth Amendment, *Missouri v. Holland*, 252 U.S. 416 (1920), the precise extent to which Congress may do so remains unclear. *See generally* Edward T. Swaine, *Does Federalism Constrain the Treaty Power?*, 103 Colum. L. Rev. 403 (2003). For criticism of the Supreme Court's decision in *Missouri v. Holland*, and arguments that the treaty power may not expand Congress's legislative power, see Nicholas Quinn Rosenkranz, *Executing the Treaty Power*, 118 Harv. L. Rev. 1867 (2005).

[138] U.S. Const., Art. VI, cl. 2.

[139] Medellin v. Texas, 552 U.S. 491 (2008). For more information *see,* CRS Report RL34450, *Can the President Compel Domestic Enforcement of an International Tribunal's Judgment? Overview of Supreme Court Decision in Medellin v. Texas*, by Michael John Garcia.

[140] Foster v. Neilson, 27 U.S. 253 (1829).

[141] *Medellin*, 552 U.S. at 505.

[142] 552 U.S. 491 (2008).

[143] *Id.* at 504-05.

[144] *Id.* at 522-23.

[145] See, e.g., 21 U.S.C. §801-801(a) ("The Convention[on Psychotropic Substances] is not self-executing, and the obligations of the United States thereunder may only be performed pursuant to appropriate legislation. It is the intent of the Congress that the amendments made by this Act, together with existing law, will enable the United States to meet all of its obligations under the Convention ...").

[146] An argument may also be forwarded that the Colorado and Washington laws should be preempted on the grounds that they interfere with the federal government's ability to conduct foreign affairs. See, American Ins. Assoc. v. Garamendi, 539 U.S. 396 (2003) (striking down the California Holocaust Victim Insurance Relief Act); Crosby v. National Foreign Trade Council, 530 U.S. 363 (2000) (invalidating a Massachusetts law targeting companies doing business in Burma). However, it would appear that a state drug law relating to the treatment of marijuana by persons within the states' jurisdiction is distinguishable from the laws at issue *Garamendi* and *Crosby*.

[147] County of San Diego v. San Diego NORML, 165 Cal. App. 4th 798, 812 n.3 (2008) ("this treaty is not self- executing, and Counties do not explain how the treaty lends any added weight to the preemption questions presented here.").

[148] For a potential exception to the general proposition that non-self-executing treaties do not have preemptive effect *see*, Safety Nat'l Cas. Corp. v. Certain Underwriters at Lloyd's, London, 587 F.3d 714 (5th Cir. 2009). In that case, a federal appellate court gave preemptive effect to an "implemented non-self-executing treaty." For a detailed discussion of the issue, *see* Leonie W. Huang, *Which Treaties Reign Supreme? The Dormant Supremacy Clause Effect of Implemented Non-Self-Executing Treaties*, 79 FORDHAM L. REV. 2211 (2011). Additional questions relating to state and federal obligations under these international drug control treaties, including the consequences of any deviation from international obligations, are beyond the scope of this report.

[149] Phil Mattingly, *Marijuana State Law Response Planned Soon, Holder Tells Panel,* BLOOMBERG, March 6, 2013, *at* http://www.bloomberg.com/news/2013-03-06/marijuana-state-law-response-planned-soon-holder-tells-panel.html.

[150] United States v. Goodwin, 457 U.S. 368, 380 (1982).

[151] Wayte v. United States, 470 U.S. 598, 607 (1985).

[152] Memorandum for selected U.S. Attorneys from David W. Ogden, Deputy Attorney General, *Investigations and Prosecutions in States Authorizing the Medical Use of Marijuana*, October 19, 2009 (hereinafter Ogden Memorandum) *available at* http://www.justice.gov/opa/documents/medical-marijuana.pdf.

[153] *Id.* at 1-2.

[154] *Id.* at 3.

[155] Memorandum for U.S. Attorneys from James M. Cole, Deputy Attorney General, *Guidance Regarding the Ogden Memo in Jurisdictions Seeking to Authorize Marijuana for Medical Use*, October 19, 2009 (hereinafter Cole Memorandum).

[156] *Id.* at 2.

[157] U.S. CONST. amend. V ("No person shall ... be deprived of ... property, without due process of law ...").

[158] For a more extensive discussion of forfeiture generally, *see* CRS Report 97-139, *Crime and Forfeiture*, by Charles Doyle.

[159] *See, e.g.,* 21 U.S.C. §881(a)(6) (proceeds), and 21 U.S.C. §881(a)(2) (products and equipment used to facilitate the offense).

[160] 21 U.S.C. §881(a) (emphasis added).

[161] 18 U.S.C. §981(b).

[162] 21 U.S.C. §881(e).

[163] 21 U.S.C. §881(e).

[164] *See, e.g.,* U.S. Dep't of Justice, *Press Release: Federal Authorities Take Enforcement Actions Against Commercial Marijuana Stores in Orange County Cities of Anaheim and La Habra,* August 21, 2012, *available at* http://www.justice.gov/usao/cac/Pressroom/2012/111.html.

[165] *See* David Downs, *City of Oakland Loses Lawsuit Against Department of Justice; Harborside Forfeiture Case Proceeds,* February 15, 2013, East Bay Express, *available at* http://www.eastbayexpress.com/LegalizationNation/ archives/2013/02/15/city-of-oakland-loses-lawsuit-against-department-of-justice-harborside-forfeiture-case-proceeds (describing how a federal magistrate judge dismissed the City of Oakland's lawsuit against Attorney General Eric Holder and U.S. Attorney Melinda Haag, which sought to prevent Haag from seizing the building leased by Harborside Health Center, one of the world's largest medical marijuana dispensaries. The judge held that only the dispensary and its landlords have legal standing to challenge the U.S. government's attempted seizure of the property.).

[166] A group of former DEA administrators have reportedly advocated for this action. See, Michael Tarm, *Ex-DEA Heads, UN Panel Urge U.S. to Nullify Pot Laws*, Associated Press, March 5, 2013.

[167] Arizona v. United States, 132 S. Ct. 2492 (2012).

[168] 18 U.S.C. §922(g)(3).

[169] 27 C.F.R. §478.11.

[170] See, Open Letter to All Federal Firearm Licensers, September 21, 2011, *available at* http://www.atf.gov/files/press/ releases/2011/09/092611-atf-open-letter-to-all-ffls-marijuana-for-medicinal-purposes.pdf.

[171] 42 U.S.C. §§13661-13662.

[172] *Id.*

[173] See, Memorandum from Helen R. Kanoovsky, Medical Use of Marijuana and Reasonable Accommodation in Federal Public and Assisted Housing, January 20, 2011, available at http://www.scribd.com/doc/47657807/HUD- policy-Memo-on-Medical-Marijuana-in-Public-Housing.

[174] 41 U.S.C. §§701 et seq.

[175] U.S. Dept. of Labor, *Drug-Free Workplace Act of 1988 Requirements, available at* http://www.dol.gov/elaws/asp/drugfree/screenr.htm.

[176] There are slightly different requirements for individuals and organizations that receive federal contracts or grants. *See* U.S. Dept. of Labor, *Drug-Free Workplace Act of 1988 Requirements for Individuals, available at* http://www.dol.gov/elaws/asp/drugfree/req_ind.htm *("Any individual who receives a contract or grant from the Federal government, regardless of dollar value, must agree not to engage in the unlawful manufacture, distribution, dispensation, possession or use of a controlled substance in the performance of this contract/grant."), and U.S. Dept. of Labor, Drug-Free Workplace Act of 1988 Requirements for Organizations, available at* http://www.dol.gov/elaws/asp/drugfree/require.htm ("All organizations covered by the Drug-Free Workplace Act of 1988 are required to provide a drug-free workplace by ... [publishing] and [giving] a policy statement to all covered employees informing them that the unlawful manufacture, distribution, dispensation, possession or use of a controlled substance is prohibited in the covered workplace and specifying the actions that will be taken against employees who violate the policy).

[177] Several state supreme courts have upheld the right of employers to discharge, or refuse to hire, employees who engage in medical marijuana use, even if such usage is allowed by state law. *See, e.g.,* Roe v. TeleTech Customer Care Mgmt. (Colo.), LLC, 257 P.3d 586 (Wash. 2011) (holding that the Washington State Medical Use of Marijuana Act does not prohibit an employer from firing an employee for physician-approved medical marijuana use). In addition, state supreme courts have ruled that employers are not required to accommodate the use of marijuana in the workplace. *See, e.g.,* Ross v. RagingWire Telecommunications, Inc., 174 P.3d 200 (Cal. 2008) (holding that nothing in the text or legislative history of California's Compassionate Use Act creates a duty on the part of employers to accommodate marijuana use by employees); Emerald Steel Fabricators, Inc. v. Bureau of Labor and Industries, 230 P.3d 518 (Or. 2010) (holding that employers have no obligations to accommodate employees' medical marijuana use).

[178] P.L. 105-244, codified at 20 U.S.C. §1011i.

[179] 29 U.S.C. §651 et seq.

[180] H.R. 499, §101(a).

[181] *Id.* §102.

[182] *Id.* §103.

[183] 27 U.S.C. §201 et seq.

[184] *Id.* §201, adding new 27 U.S.C. §301.

[185] *Id.* §301.

[186] *Id.* §302.

[187] H.R. 501, §2(a), adding new 26 U.S.C. §5901.

[188] The bill defines "marijuana enterprise" as a producer, importer, manufacturer, distributor, retailer, or any person who transports, stores, displays, or otherwise participates in any

business activity that handles marijuana or marijuana products. *Id.* §2(a), adding new 26 U.S.C. §5904(8).

[189] *Id.* §2(a), adding new 26 U.S.C. §5911.

[190] *Id.* §2(a), adding new 26 U.S.C. §5912.

[191] *Id.* §2(a), adding new 26 U.S.C. §§5921, 5922.

[192] H.R. 689, §2(a)(1).

[193] *Id.* §2(a)(2).

[194] 21 U.S.C. §301 et seq.

[195] H.R. 689, §§2(b), (3).

[196] *Id.* §4.

[197] *Id.*

[198] H.R. 710, §2(a), adding new 18 U.S.C. §§3436(a), (b)(1).

[199] *Id.* §2(a), adding new 18 U.S.C. §3436(c).

[200] *Id.* §2(a), adding new 18 U.S.C. §3436(b)(2).

[201] 21 U.S.C. §881.

[202] H.R. 784, §3, amending section 511(a) of the CSA (21 U.S.C. §881(a)(7)).

[203] H.R. 964, §2, amending Section 708 of the CSA (21 U.S.C. §903).

In: Recreational and Medical Marijuana
Editors: Valentin Dijkstra
ISBN: 978-1-62808-114-5

Chapter 2

MEDICAL MARIJUANA: THE SUPREMACY CLAUSE, FEDERALISM, AND THE INTERPLAY BETWEEN STATE AND FEDERAL LAWS*

Todd Garvey

SUMMARY

As part of a larger scheme to regulate drugs and other controlled substances, federal law prohibits the cultivation, distribution, and possession of marijuana. No exception is made for marijuana used in the course of a recommended medical treatment. Indeed, by categorizing marijuana as a Schedule I drug under the Controlled Substances Act (CSA), the federal government has concluded that marijuana has "no currently accepted medical use in treatment in the United States." Yet 18 states and the District of Columbia have decriminalized medical marijuana by enacting exceptions to their state drug laws that permit individuals to grow, possess, or use marijuana for medicinal purposes. In contrast to the complete federal prohibition, these 19 jurisdictions see medicinal value in marijuana and permit the drug's use under certain circumstances.

Although the U.S. Supreme Court has established Congress's constitutional authority to enact the existing federal prohibition on marijuana,

* This is an edited, reformatted and augmented version of the Congressional Research Service Publication, CRS Report for Congress R42398, dated November 9, 2012.

principles of federalism prevent the federal government from mandating that the states actively support or participate in enforcing the federal law. While state resources may be helpful in combating the illegal use of marijuana, Congress's ability to compel the states to enact similar criminal prohibitions, to repeal medical marijuana exemptions, or to direct state police officers to enforce the federal law remains limited by the Tenth Amendment.

Even if the federal government is prohibited from mandating that the states adopt laws supportive of federal policy, the constitutional doctrine of preemption generally prevents states from enacting laws that are inconsistent with federal law. Under the Supremacy Clause, state laws that conflict with federal law are generally preempted and therefore void. Courts, however, have not viewed the relationship between state and federal marijuana laws in such a manner, nor did Congress intend that the CSA displace all state laws associated with controlled substances. Instead, the relationship between the federal ban on marijuana and state medical marijuana exemptions must be considered in the context of two distinct sovereigns, each enacting separate and independent criminal regimes with separate and independent enforcement mechanisms, in which certain conduct may be prohibited under one sovereign and not the other. Although state and federal marijuana laws may be "logically inconsistent," a decision not to criminalize—or even to expressly decriminalize—conduct for purposes of the law within one sphere does nothing to alter the legality of that same conduct in the other sphere.

This report will review the federal government's constitutional authority to enact the federal criminal prohibition on marijuana; highlight certain principles of federalism that prevent the federal government from mandating that states participate in enforcing the federal prohibition; consider unresolved questions relating to the extent to which state authorization and regulation of medical marijuana are preempted by federal law; and assess what obligations, if any, the U.S. Department of Justice (DOJ) has to investigate and prosecute violations of the federal prohibition on marijuana.

INTRODUCTION

As part of a larger scheme to regulate drugs and other controlled substances, federal law prohibits the cultivation, distribution, and possession of marijuana.[1] No exception is made for marijuana used in the course of a recommended medical treatment. Indeed, by categorizing marijuana as a

Schedule I drug under the Controlled Substances Act (CSA), the federal government has concluded that marijuana has "no currently accepted medical use in treatment in the United States."[2]

Yet 18 states and the District of Columbia have decriminalized medical marijuana by enacting exceptions to their drug laws that permit individuals to grow, possess, or use marijuana for medicinal purposes.[3] In contrast to the complete federal prohibition, these 19 jurisdictions see medicinal value in marijuana and permit the drug's use under certain circumstances. Such inconsistencies in federal and state law would generally evoke the constitutional principle of preemption—potentially resulting in a conclusion that because the states permit conduct that the federal government has expressly prohibited, such laws are void as in conflict with the "supreme law of the land."[4] This, however, has not been the case. State laws that exempt from state criminal sanctions the cultivation, distribution, or possession of marijuana for medical purposes have generally not been preempted by federal law.

This unique interplay between state and federal law has led to a seemingly incongruous situation in which both the federal criminal prohibition on marijuana and state medical marijuana exemptions coexist. Accordingly, a resident of California who uses marijuana for medical purposes in compliance with California law is nonetheless simultaneously in violation of federal law and potentially subject to prosecution by federal authorities. Such prosecutions, however, are relatively rare. The federal government has limited resources to draw upon in investigating and enforcing federal drug laws.[5] As a consequence, the Obama Administration has formally suggested that it will not prosecute individuals who use medicinal marijuana in a manner consistent with state laws.[6]

The legal anomaly that defines the use of medical marijuana in the United States raises a number of important constitutional questions—some of which have been answered by the U.S. Supreme Court, but many of which remain unresolved. This report will review the federal government's constitutional authority to enact the federal criminal prohibition on marijuana; highlight certain principles of federalism that prevent the federal government from mandating that states participate in enforcing the federal prohibition; consider unresolved questions relating to the extent to which state authorization and regulation of medical marijuana are preempted by federal law; and assess what obligations, if any, the U.S. Department of Justice (DOJ) has to investigate and prosecute violations of the federal prohibition on marijuana.

LEGAL LANDSCAPE: FEDERAL AND STATE LAWS

Prior to considering the significant constitutional questions associated with the interplay between state and federal laws in the context of medical marijuana, the following section provides a description of the CSA and a brief discussion of common characteristics found within the wide variety of state medical marijuana laws that have been enacted across the country.

Federal Law

Enacted in 1970, the CSA establishes a statutory framework through which the federal government regulates the lawful production, possession, and distribution of controlled substances.[7] The CSA places various plants, drugs, and chemicals (such as narcotics, stimulants, depressants, hallucinogens, and anabolic steroids) into one of five schedules based on the substance's medical use, potential for abuse, and safety or dependence liability.[8] Further, the act requires persons who handle controlled substances or listed chemicals (such as drug manufacturers, wholesale distributors, doctors, hospitals, pharmacies, and scientific researchers) to register with the Drug Enforcement Administration (DEA) in DOJ, which administers and enforces the CSA.[9] Registrants must maintain detailed records of their respective controlled substance inventories, as well as establish adequate security controls to minimize theft and diversion.[10]

Marijuana is currently categorized as a Schedule I controlled substance, and is therefore subject to the most severe restrictions contained within the CSA. Schedule I drugs have "a high potential for abuse" and "no currently accepted medical use in treatment in the United States," and lack "accepted safety for use of the drug [] under medical supervisions."[11] Pursuant to the CSA, the cultivation, distribution, or possession of marijuana is a federal crime.[12] Although various factors contribute to the ultimate sentence received, the mere possession of marijuana generally constitutes a misdemeanor subject to up to one year imprisonment and a minimum fine of $1,000.[13] The cultivation or distribution of marijuana, or the possession of marijuana with the intent to distribute, on the other hand, is subject to more severe penalties. Such conduct generally constitutes a felony subject to as much as five years imprisonment and a fine of up to $250,000.[14]

Although individuals who use medical marijuana in compliance with state law are still in violation of federal law and subject to prosecution by federal authorities at any time, the Obama Administration has announced an informal policy that suggests a federal prosecution in that situation would be unlikely. In an October 19, 2009, memorandum, Deputy Attorney General David W. Ogden provided guidance to federal prosecutors in states that have authorized the use of medical marijuana.[15] Citing a desire to make "efficient and rational use of its limited investigative and prosecutorial resources," the memorandum stated that while the "prosecution of significant traffickers of illegal drugs, including marijuana ... continues to be a core priority," federal prosecutors "should not focus federal resources [] on individuals whose actions are in clear and unambiguous compliance with existing state laws providing for the medical use of marijuana."[16] The memorandum made clear, however, that "this guidance [does not] preclude investigation or prosecution, even where there is clear and unambiguous compliance with existing state law, in particular circumstances where investigation or prosecution otherwise serves important federal interests."[17]

Responding to an increase in the "commercial cultivation, sale, distribution, and use of marijuana for purported medical purposes," DOJ released a subsequent memorandum in 2011 drawing a clear distinction between the potential prosecutions of individual patients who require marijuana in the course of medical treatment and "commercial" dispensaries.[18] After noting that several jurisdictions had recently "enacted legislation to authorize multiple large-scale, privately operated industrial marijuana cultivation centers," DOJ attempted to clarify the scope of the Ogden Memorandum:

> The Ogden memorandum was never intended to shield such activities from federal enforcement action and prosecution, even where those activities purport to comply with state law. Persons who are in the business of cultivating, selling or distributing marijuana, and those who knowingly facilitate such activities, are in violation of the [CSA] regardless of state law. Consistent with resource constraints and the discretion you may exercise in your district, such persons are subject to federal enforcement action, including potential prosecution.[19]

The memorandum clearly communicated that individuals operating or "facilitating" medical marijuana dispensaries, even if operated in compliance with state law, continue to be targets for federal prosecution. As a result, the last two years have seen a reported increase in the number of federal DEA raids on dispensaries and marijuana farms and the subsequent prosecutions of those who own and operate marijuana distribution facilities.[20] Additionally, a number of states have abandoned legislative proposals to expand their medical marijuana programs, at least partly as a result of warnings from U.S. Attorneys that the DOJ will "vigorously" enforce the CSA against those who participate in the unlawful manufacturing or distribution of marijuana, regardless of whether such activity is licensed under state law.[21]

State Laws

Forty-eight states and the District of Columbia have criminalized the recreational use of marijuana.[22] However, beginning with California in 1996, a growing number of states have decriminalized the use of marijuana for medicinal purposes or exempted qualified users from sanctions imposed under state law. Today, 18 states and the District of Columbia have enacted provisions that, in various ways, exempt qualified individuals[23] from state criminal prosecution and various state civil penalties for marijuana-related offenses.[24] Although these laws vary widely in their approaches to medical marijuana, there are a number of common characteristics that appear to adhere to these laws. First, in order for an individual to legally use medical marijuana, the drug must have been recommended by a physician for use in treating a diagnosed medical condition.[25] All states but California require that this recommendation be in writing.[26] Most states also require potential users to register with the state.[27] Upon registration, states will often provide the user with a registration card so that the individual can be identified as a qualified user of medical marijuana.[28] Additionally, all states but California limit the quantity of marijuana that a patient may possess at any one time, and most states have laws limiting the manner and place in which a qualified individual can use the drug.[29]

Although these 19 jurisdictions have established a scheme by which qualified individuals may legally possess and use marijuana for medicinal purposes under state law, qualified users in some jurisdictions lack a legal avenue to obtain adequate quantities of the drug. Some states permit users to grow their own marijuana, while others license third-party private persons or entities to cultivate and distribute the drug to qualified individuals through state-licensed and -regulated dispensaries.[30] California has also authorized patients and caregivers to collectively grow marijuana in "cannabis cooperatives."[31] In those states where supply is limited, however, many medical marijuana users are forced to acquire the marijuana they are permitted to possess and use through the black market.[32]

A Series of Constitutional Questions

The unique inconsistencies between federal and state approaches to medical marijuana give rise to a series of important constitutional questions. First, is it within Congress's power to prohibit the production, possession, and distribution of marijuana? Second, to what extent can the federal government direct states to adopt similar laws or enforce the federal prohibition? Third, to what extent are state attempts to authorize and regulate medical marijuana preempted by federal law? And finally, what obligation, if any, does DOJ have to enforce the federal prohibition?

Is It Within Congress's Power to Prohibit the Production, Possession, and Distribution of Marijuana?

The U.S. Supreme Court considered the reach of Congress's Commerce Clause authority and the constitutionality of the CSA in *Gonzales v. Raich*.[33] *Raich* involved a challenge to the federal marijuana prohibition brought by Angel Raich and Diane Monson after agents of the federal DEA seized and destroyed marijuana plants that Monson had been cultivating for medical purposes consistent with California law. The respondents argued that the CSA's "categorical prohibition," as applied to the "intrastate manufacture and possession of marijuana for medical purposes," exceeded Congress's authority under the Commerce Clause, and, therefore, could not serve as the basis for their prosecution.[34] The Court rejected this argument, and clearly held that the federal prohibition was within Congress's constitutional authority.

In a 6-3 decision, the Court upheld Congress's power to prohibit even the purely intrastate cultivation and possession of marijuana. Relying heavily on its 1942 decision of *Wickard v. Filburn*, the Court held that prior precedent had "firmly establish[ed] Congress'[s] power to regulate purely local activities that are part of an economic 'class of activities' that have a substantial effect on interstate commerce."[35] In enacting the CSA, Congress had sought to regulate the supply and demand of controlled substances, including marijuana. Consistent with that objective, Congress had rationally concluded that "leaving home-consumed marijuana outside federal control" would have a "substantial effect on supply and demand in the national market" for marijuana.[36] The Court noted that even small amounts of marijuana grown at home— though intended for personal medicinal use—would likely be diverted into the national market and frustrate Congress's goal of strictly controlling overall supply.[37] Thus, in enacting the federal prohibition on marijuana production, possession, and distribution, Congress was acting "well within its authority to 'make all Laws which shall be necessary and proper' to 'regulate commerce ... among the several states.'"[38]

For purposes of this report, it is important to note that the Court's opinion in *Raich* dealt only with the question of whether the Commerce Clause permitted Congress to prohibit the wholly intrastate possession and use of marijuana. The Court did not consider the question of whether the California law, which permitted the use of marijuana for medicinal purposes, was preempted by the CSA. The Court noted only that respondents' compliance with state law in cultivating marijuana had no impact on the scope of Congress's power under the Commerce Clause, as "[i]t is beyond peradventure that federal power over commerce is 'superior to that of the States to provide for the welfare or necessities of their inhabitants,' however legitimate or dire those necessities may be."[39]

May the Federal Government Direct the States to Adopt Similar Laws or to Enforce the Federal Prohibition?

Although *Raich* established Congress's constitutional authority to enact the existing federal prohibition on marijuana, principles of federalism prevent the federal government from mandating that the states support or participate in enforcing the federal law. While state resources may be helpful in combating the illegal use of marijuana, Congress's ability to compel the states to enact similar criminal prohibitions, to repeal medical marijuana exemptions, or to direct state police officers to enforce the federal law remains limited. The Tenth Amendment likely prevents such an intrusion into state sovereignty.

The Tenth Amendment provides that the "powers not delegated to the United States by the Constitution, nor prohibited by it to the States, are reserved to the States respectively, or to the people."[40] Initially, the Supreme Court interpreted the Tenth Amendment as establishing that certain "core" state functions would be beyond the authority of the federal government to regulate.[41] The Court's interpretation of the Tenth Amendment soon shifted, however, from protecting "core" state functions to preventing the federal government from "commandeering" state government.[42] In *New York v. United States*, the Court struck down a federal statute that had mandated that states either develop legislation on how to dispose of all low-level radioactive waste generated within their borders, or be forced to take title to such waste and become responsible for any financial consequences.[43] The Court found that although Congress had the authority under the Commerce Clause to regulate low-level radioactive waste, it had only the power to regulate the waste directly—Congress could not require that the states perform the regulation rather than regulate the waste directly itself. In effect, Congress could not "commandeer" the legislative process of the states.[44]

Nor may Congress "commandeer" state executive branch officers for purposes of carrying out or enforcing federal law. In *Printz v. United States*, the Supreme Court invalidated a provision of the Brady Handgun Violence Prevention Act that had required that state police officers conduct background checks on prospective handgun purchasers within five days of an attempted purchase.[45] The Court held that the provision constituted an unconstitutional "commandeering" of state officers and, like a commandeering of the legislature, was outside of Congress's power and a violation of the Tenth Amendment.[46]

Consistent with *New York v. United States* and *Printz*, the federal government is prohibited from commandeering state legislatures or state executive officials by mandating that states enact certain legislation or implement or enforce a federal law.[47] Given these restrictions, Congress may not statutorily direct that states enact complete prohibitions on marijuana or repeal existing exemptions for medical marijuana. Nor may Congress direct that state police officers enforce the marijuana provisions of the CSA. Congress may, however, be able to persuade states to support the federal policy by conditioning the receipt of federal funds upon the state enacting legislation consistent with the CSA.[48] In addition, states may voluntarily alter their own laws or enforce federal laws, but they cannot be made to do so by the federal government.[49]

To What Extent Are State Medical Marijuana Laws Preempted by Federal Law?

Even if the federal government is prohibited from mandating that the states adopt laws supportive of federal policy, the constitutional doctrine of preemption generally prevents states from enacting laws that are inconsistent with federal law. Thus, the federal government typically stands on much stronger constitutional footing when it attempts to stop a state action than when it attempts to force a state to act.

At first glance, it would appear that a state law that permits an activity expressly prohibited by federal law would necessarily create a legal "conflict" between state and federal law. Under the Supremacy Clause, state laws that conflict with federal law are generally preempted and therefore void.[50] Courts, however, have not viewed the relationship between state and federal marijuana laws in such a manner, nor did Congress intend that the CSA displace all state laws associated with controlled substances.[51] Instead, the relationship between the federal ban on marijuana and state medical marijuana exemptions must be considered in the context of two distinct sovereigns, each enacting separate and independent criminal regimes with separate and independent enforcement mechanisms, in which certain conduct may be prohibited under one sovereign and not the other. Although state and federal marijuana laws may be "logically inconsistent," a decision not to criminalize—or even to expressly decriminalize—conduct for purposes of the law within one sphere does nothing to alter the legality of that same conduct in the other sphere.

Preemption is grounded in the Supremacy Clause of Article VI, cl. 2, which states that "[t]he Constitution, and the Laws of the United States which shall be made in Pursuance thereof; and all Treaties made, or which shall be made, under the Authority of the United States, shall be the supreme Law of the Land."[52] The Supremacy Clause, therefore, "elevates" the U.S. Constitution, federal statutes, federal regulations, and ratified treaties above the laws of the states.[53] As a result, where a state law is in conflict with a federal law, the federal law must prevail. There is, however, a presumption against federal preemption when it comes to the exercise of "historic police powers of the States."[54] State medical marijuana laws have generally been accorded this presumption, as they are enacted pursuant to traditional state police powers in defining criminal conduct and regulating drugs and medical practices.

Although there is "no one crystal clear distinctly marked formula" for determining whether a state law is preempted by federal law, the Supreme Court has established three general classes of preemption: express preemption, conflict preemption, and field preemption.[55] In each instance, however, "the question of preemption is one of determining congressional intent."[56] Express preemption exists where the language of a federal statute explicitly states the degree to which related state laws are superseded by the federal statute.[57] Where, in contrast, Congress does not articulate its view as to a statute's intended impact on state laws, a court may *imply* preemption if there is evidence that Congress intended to supplant state authority.[58] Preemption is generally implied in two situations. First, under conflict preemption, a state law is preempted "where compliance with both federal law and state regulations is a physical impossibility ... or where state law stands as an obstacle to the accomplishment and execution of the full purposes and objectives of Congress."[59] Thus, where one cannot simultaneously comply with both state and federal law, or where the state law directly frustrates the purpose of a federal law, the state law is preempted. Second, under field preemption, a state law is preempted where a "scheme of federal regulation is so pervasive as to make reasonable the inference that Congress left no room for the States to supplement it.... "[60]

The CSA contains a statutory preemption provision that expressly articulates Congress's intent as to the relationship between state and federal law and the extent to which the latter displaces the former. Section 903 states:

> No provision of this subchapter shall be construed as indicating an intent on the part of the Congress to occupy the field in which that provision operates, including criminal penalties, to the exclusion of any State law on the same subject matter which would otherwise be within the authority of the State, *unless there is a positive conflict between that provision of this subchapter and that State law so that the two cannot consistently stand together.*[61]

The CSA's preemptive effect is therefore limited to only those state laws that are in "positive conflict" with the CSA such that the two "cannot consistently stand together."[62] Notably, the provision clarifies that Congress did not intend to entirely occupy the regulatory field concerning controlled substances or wholly supplant traditional state authority in the area. Indeed, Congress expressly declined to assert field preemption as grounds for preempting state law under the CSA. Arguably, then, the preemptive effect of the CSA is not as broad as congressional authority could have allowed. States remain free to pass laws relating to marijuana, or other controlled substances, so long as they do not create a "positive conflict" with federal law. In interpreting this provision, courts have generally established that a state medical marijuana law is in "positive conflict" with the CSA if it is "physically impossible" to comply with both the state and federal law, or where the state law "stands as an obstacle to the accomplishment and execution of the full purposes and objectives of Congress."[63]

CSA Preemption as Applied to State Medical Marijuana Exemptions

Both federal and state courts have consistently held that a state's decision to exempt certain classes of individuals from the state prohibition on marijuana by permitting the drug's use for medicinal purposes does not create a "positive conflict" with federal law. A mere exemption from state prosecution neither (1) makes it "impossible to comply" with both state and federal law nor (2) "stands as an obstacle" to the execution of Congress's objectives.

The "impossibility" prong of conflict preemption has traditionally been viewed very narrowly. The Supreme Court has consistently held that there is no basis to imply impossibility preemption where a state simply *permits* what the federal government *prohibits*.[64] So long as an individual is not compelled to engage in conduct prohibited by federal law, then simultaneous compliance with both laws is not impossible.[65] In the medical marijuana context, an individual can comply with the CSA and a state medical marijuana exemption by refraining from the use of marijuana altogether. Under established precedent, it would appear that the federal prohibition on marijuana would only preempt a state medical marijuana law under the impossibility prong of conflict preemption if the state law *required* individuals to use medical marijuana. State laws, of course, contain no such mandate.

The second prong of the conflict preemption analysis is broader in scope. State laws may be deemed to be in conflict with federal law if the state law "stands as an obstacle to the accomplishment and execution of the full purposes and objectives of Congress."[66] In applying this test, the Supreme Court has stated that a reviewing court must consider congressional intent and the "purposes and objectives" of the federal statute as a whole.[67] "If the purpose of the act cannot otherwise be accomplished," the Court has held, then "the state law must yield to the regulation of Congress …"[68] Additionally, the Court has established that in areas of traditional state concern—an area within which medical marijuana laws likely fall—there exists a presumption against preemption.[69] In these areas, a more "significant" conflict may be required before a state law constitutes an obstacle to the achievement of the federal goal.[70]

Courts have generally viewed state medical marijuana exemptions as having only a limited impact on the federal government's ability to achieve its purpose of combating the use of marijuana pursuant to the CSA. An exemption from prosecution under state law does not obstruct the federal government's ability to investigate and prosecute an individual for a violation of federal law.[71] Federal courts have consistently held that compliance with state medical marijuana laws is no defense, and provides no immunity to a federal criminal prosecution under the CSA.[72] Indeed, in hearing a prosecution under federal law, at least one federal court has gone so far as to exclude the introduction of any evidence relating to the defendant's compliance with state medical marijuana provisions.[73]

While an argument can be made that the decriminalization of medical marijuana under state law represents an "obstacle to the accomplishment ... of the full purposes and objectives of Congress" by creating confusion as to the permissible uses of marijuana, it is not the case that the federal objectives "cannot otherwise be accomplished" in the face of state medical marijuana exemptions.[74] The federal government is still free to expend its own resources to implement and enforce its own law. Moreover, if a state decision to not criminalize conduct otherwise prohibited by federal law qualified as an obstacle to the accomplishment of federal objectives, then obstacle preemption would effectively amount to an impermissible "license to commandeer state or local resources" by denying states the ability to treat certain conduct differently than the federal government.[75]

CSA Preemption as Applied to State Authorizations of Medical Marijuana

With most state medical marijuana exemptions surviving preemption challenges, various states have utilized the resulting momentum to attempt to exert increased state control over the use of medical marijuana within their borders. As a result, some state laws have evolved from merely exempting qualified individuals from prosecution under state drug laws, to affirmatively authorizing and regulating the use of medical marijuana. For example, whereas California's initial medical marijuana law only decriminalized the use of marijuana for medicinal purposes, the state expanded its law in 2003 under the Medical Marijuana Program Act.[76] The law required that the California Department of Public Health establish a voluntary registration and identification system, under which all California counties were required to issue state identification cards to qualified applicants.[77] The law also authorized qualified individuals and primary caregivers to possess up to 8 ounces of marijuana and 6 mature marijuana plants—a provision that was later struck down by the California Supreme Court.[78] Moreover, California now permits the formation of cooperatives through which qualified individuals can cultivate and distribute marijuana.[79]

Although it is difficult to determine the extent to which states can legalize and regulate medical marijuana, laws that exceed a decision not to criminalize specific conduct, and instead actively authorize the use of marijuana in contravention of the CSA, would appear to raise more stark preemption concerns. For example, a state law that attempted to immunize its citizens from federal prosecution would be preempted as a direct obstacle to the accomplishment of federal objectives. So, too, would a state law that sought to protect its citizens from the consequences of marijuana use, such as potential disqualification from public housing, under other federal statutes.[80] Additionally, a strong argument can probably be made that if a state were to enact a law through which the state itself cultivated and distributed marijuana to qualified individuals, such a law would also be preempted.[81] Whether other, less intrusive, state laws may also be preempted remains uncertain.

It does not appear that any federal court has engaged in a substantial discussion of the preemption issues associated with these increasingly expansive state laws.[82] However, in order to highlight the difficulty in delineating the preemptive scope of the CSA, it may be helpful to consider two state cases reviewing the California and Oregon state registration and identification card programs. These laws permit a qualified individual to register with the state and receive an identification card that is used to identify the individual as one who is permitted to cultivate or possess marijuana.[83] In analyzing whether this type of law is preempted by the CSA, the California and Oregon courts have reached very different results.

State-Issued Identification Card Program Not Preempted

In *County of San Diego v. San Diego Norml*, a California appellate court upheld the registration and identification card provisions of the California Medical Marijuana Program Act (MMPA).[84] Challenging the law, San Diego County argued that the provisions of the MMPA which required the county to issue identification cards to qualified patients and primary caregivers were preempted by the CSA and therefore without effect.[85]

In considering the preemption issue, the California court first attempted to define the preemptive scope of the CSA. Interpreting Section 903 of the CSA, the court concluded that Congress had demonstrated its intent to reject both express and field preemption—leaving only conflict preemption as sufficient to preempt a state marijuana law.[86] Notably, after considering the previously discussed "impossibility" and "obstacle" prongs of conflict preemption, the court concluded that the language of the CSA suggested that Congress "did not intend to supplant all laws posing some conceivable obstacle to the purposes of the CSA."[87] Thus, the court rejected the application of "obstacle" preemption under the CSA and held that a state law should only be preempted if it were impossible to simultaneously comply with both state and federal law.

Although determining that obstacle preemption was not applicable under the CSA, the court went on to hold that even if Congress had intended to preempt state laws that made compliance with federal law impossible or that represented an obstacle to the achievement of federal objectives, the California identification laws would still not be preempted under either standard.[88] In reaching this conclusion, the court noted that the identification cards did not "insulate the bearer from federal laws," nor did the card "imply the holder is immune from prosecution for federal offenses."[89] The identification cards, the court reasoned, instead represented a "mechanism" by which California law enforcement officers could efficiently identify those individuals who are exempted from prosecution under California law for their use of marijuana.[90]

State-Issued Identification Card Program Preempted

Contrary to the California holding, in *Emerald Steel Fabricators v. Bureau of Labor and Industries*, the Oregon Supreme Court concluded that similar identification card provisions in the Oregon Medical Marijuana Act were in "positive conflict" with the CSA and therefore preempted.[91] Under Oregon law, the state issues qualified individuals identification cards that authorize the individual to "engage in the medical use … of marijuana" without the threat of state prosecution.[92] The challenge to the law arose in the context of an employment discrimination claim in which an employee, who had obtained an identification card due to a medical condition, was allegedly discharged for admitting that he used marijuana.[93] Oregon law requires that employers "make reasonable accommodations" for an employee's disability as long as such an accommodation does not impose an undue hardship upon the employer.[94] However, the law is to be interpreted consistently with the federal Americans with Disabilities Act, which does not afford protections for employees "currently engaged in the illegal use of drugs."[95] Although the employee's use of marijuana was legal under state law, the employer argued that the medicinal use of marijuana remains illegal under federal law and that "to the extent that [Oregon law] affirmatively authorizes the use of medical marijuana, federal law preempts that subsection …"[96]

Unlike the California court, the Oregon Supreme Court concluded that if a state law fell within either the "impossibility" prong or the "obstacle" prong of the conflict preemption analysis, then the state law would be preempted by the CSA.[97] Noting that the Supreme Court has applied the impossibility prong of the analysis "narrowly," the court first determined that an individual could simultaneously comply with both the state and federal law by refraining from the use of marijuana.[98] However, in turning to the obstacle prong, the court held that because the Oregon law "affirmatively authorized the use of medical marijuana," it was preempted by the CSA. The court reasoned that while the law did not prevent the federal government from enforcing its own laws against Oregon users, by "affirmatively authorizing a use that federal law prohibits," the Oregon law "stands as an obstacle to the implementation and execution of the full purposes and objectives of the Controlled Substances Act."[99] Although the court concluded that the state provisions that exempted medical marijuana users from criminal liability were within the states' authority and beyond the reach of Congress under the Tenth Amendment, the licensing provision—which authorizes an individual with an identification card to engage in the use of marijuana—was distinguishable.[100] "There is no dispute," held the court, "that Congress has the authority under the Supremacy Clause to preempt state laws that affirmatively authorize the use of medical marijuana."[101]

County of San Diego and *Emerald Steel* display the apparent ambiguities associated with delineating the degree to which states can address medical marijuana within their borders. These cases highlight a number of important questions that may play a significant role in how other courts approach these preemption questions. First, will other courts adopt the Oregon Supreme Court's distinction between a permissible "exemption" and an impermissible "authorization"?[102] If so, the consequences of such an approach could be significant. Second, should state licensing laws be characterized as an affirmative state authorization to use marijuana, or merely a mechanism by which state law enforcement officers can identify a specific class of individuals who qualify for the state medical marijuana exemption? These questions, and others, remain unresolved. However, even if state laws were not preempted, the growth of state medical marijuana laws will likely still be limited by the degree to which the federal government is willing to prosecute violations of the CSA.

Liability for State Officials?

It should be noted that state laws that provide a mechanism by which state officials who participate in helping qualified individuals gain access to marijuana may theoretically expose those state officials to federal criminal liability. It is not only individuals who possess, produce, or distribute marijuana who are subject to federal sanctions, but also those who conspire, aid and abet, or assist in that proscribed conduct.[103] Take for example, state laws that require state officials to return marijuana improperly seized from a qualified individual.[104] Theoretically, the action of returning that marijuana would qualify as a felony distribution of marijuana under the CSA. Although the CSA contains language that may act to protect state officials, the precise impact of the provision remains unclear. Section 885 provides that "no civil or criminal liability shall be imposed ... upon any duly authorized officer of any state ... who shall be lawfully engaged in the enforcement of any law ... relating to controlled substances."[105] This provision may provide protections for state officials carrying out state-directed actions that are in contravention of the CSA.[106]

In contrast, however, the U.S. Attorneys for the Eastern and Western Districts of Washington State have expressly noted that state officials could be subject to prosecution under federal law for carrying out aspects of a state medical marijuana program that violates the CSA.[107] In response to a request for DOJ's position on a proposed expansion to the medical marijuana laws of Washington State, these U.S. Attorneys suggested that "state employees who conducted activities mandated by the Washington legislative proposals would not be immune from liability under the CSA."[108] The letter reportedly played a role in the governor's decision to veto the proposal.

The state of Arizona recently asked a federal district court to resolve the state officer immunity question. Partially out of concern for the potential criminal liability of state employees who implement state law, the governor of Arizona sought guidance from the Arizona United States Attorney's Office on whether the Arizona Medical Marijuana Act created a "safe harbor" from federal prosecution under the CSA. Although not referencing state employees specifically, the U.S. Attorney for the District of Arizona responded with a letter informing the governor that "growing, distributing, and possessing marijuana violates federal law no matter what state law permits," and that "compliance with state law does not create a 'safe harbor.'"[109]

The state filed suit in the U.S. District Court for the District of Arizona, asking the court for a declaratory judgment as to whether the state law created a safe harbor for state officials under the CSA. Without reaching the merits, the court dismissed the claim as unripe, holding that the state could not show that officials were "subject to a genuine threat of imminent prosecution."[110] In reaching this holding, the court specifically noted that plaintiffs had failed to "detail any history of prosecution of state employees for participation in state medical marijuana licensing schemes."[111]

What Obligation, If Any, Does the U.S. Department of Justice Have to Enforce the Federal Prohibition on Marijuana?

Although the production, possession, or distribution of marijuana is a crime under federal law, DOJ has broad discretion in deciding whether to prosecute specific violations of the law. As previously discussed, DOJ has announced a policy that federal prosecutors "should not focus federal resources [] on individuals whose actions are in clear and unambiguous compliance with existing state laws providing for the medical use of marijuana."[112] Although recognizing that the conduct remains a violation of federal law, DOJ appears to have made a decision that prosecuting individual patients who are using marijuana for medicinal purposes is not an agency priority.

The established doctrine of "prosecutorial discretion" provides the federal government with "broad discretion" as to when, whom, and whether to prosecute for violations of federal law.[113] In granting this discretion, the courts have recognized that the "decision to prosecute is particularly ill-suited to judicial review," as it involves the consideration of factors—such as the strength of evidence, deterrence value, and existing enforcement priorities—"not readily susceptible to the kind of analysis the courts are competent to undertake."[114] Although prosecutorial discretion is subject to very few limitations, it is not "unfettered." For example, the selection of whom to prosecute is subject to the non-discrimination restrictions of the Equal Protection Clause.[115] Accordingly, prosecutors cannot base a decision to prosecute on "an unjustifiable standard such as race, religion, or other arbitrary classification."[116]

A decision by an individual prosecutor not to bring charges against an individual for violating the CSA's prohibition on the production, possession, or distribution of marijuana—assuming that decision is not grounded in a discriminatory purpose—would clearly fall within the umbrella of "prosecutorial discretion." Thus, there would appear to be no constitutional defect in a prosecutor's decision not to investigate or prosecute individuals who use marijuana for medicinal purposes in compliance with state law. DOJ has no obligation to prosecute all violations of federal law.[117]

Given DOJ's position, questions may be raised as to the extent to which DOJ may decline to enforce a duly enacted federal statute. For example, a formal decision to never prosecute specific conduct that Congress has expressly disallowed may raise constitutional concerns under the separation of powers.[118] However, DOJ's position, as established in the Ogden

Memorandum, does not appear to rise to such a repudiation of existing laws—either in its form or its scope. Rather, the decision to limit prosecutions appears to be based on enforcement priorities and the allocation of resources. Indeed, the Ogden Memorandum, in conjunction with the later Cole Memorandum, specifically states that the DOJ will continue to prosecute certain violations and, in fact, has done so.

CONCLUSION

The legal status of state laws respecting the use of medical marijuana remains ambiguous. Although state laws that merely exempt qualified users of medical marijuana from state prosecution have consistently survived preemption challenges, state laws that affirmatively authorize and regulate medical marijuana may pose a more serious "obstacle" to the accomplishment of federal objectives. Notwithstanding the many unresolved questions of preemption, this interplay between state and federal law has prompted a unique legal result. While an individual may be able to possess, distribute, or cultivate marijuana for limited purposes under state law, that same conduct remains a criminal offense under federal law. For example, operators of licensed marijuana dispensaries—which may represent legitimate licensed business ventures under state law—are subject to felony prosecutions under federal law at any time. Thus, it appears that it is generally the discretionary restraint of the federal government, in addition to the necessity to prioritize limited resources, that brings some modicum of stability to the interplay between state medical marijuana laws and the federal prohibition on the production, possession, and distribution of marijuana.

End Notes

[1] Controlled Substances Act, 21 U.S.C. §§801 et seq.

[2] 21 U.S.C. §812(b)(1).

[3] Theses states include Alaska, Arizona, California, Colorado, Connecticut, Delaware, Hawaii, Maine, Massachusetts, Michigan, Montana, Nevada, New Jersey, New Mexico, Oregon, Rhode Island, Vermont, and Washington. In addition, the state of Maryland has a medical marijuana law that permits individuals arrested for possession of one ounce of marijuana or less to raise medical use as an affirmative defense at trial. Md. Ann. Code §5-601.

[4] U.S. Const., Art. VI, cl. 2 ("The Constitution, and the Laws of the United States which shall be made in Pursuance thereof; and all Treaties made, or which shall be made, under the Authority of the United States, shall be the supreme Law of the Land.").

[5] Memorandum for selected U.S. Attorneys from David W. Ogden, Deputy Attorney General, *Investigations and Prosecutions in States Authorizing the Medical Use of Marijuana*, October 19, 2009 (hereinafter Ogden Memorandum) *available at* http://www.justice.gov/opa/documents/medical-marijuana.pdf.

[6] *Id.*

[7] 21 U.S.C. §812. It should also be noted that the United States has treaty obligations to maintain effective controls over marijuana. *See, e.g.*, Single Convention on Narcotics Drugs, March 30, 1961, 18 U.S.T. 1409.

[8] 21 U.S.C. §§811-812.

[9] 21 U.S.C. §823.

[10] *See* 21 C.F.R. §1304.11(a) ("Each inventory shall contain a complete and accurate record of all controlled substances on hand ..."); *see also* 21 C.F.R. §1301.74(a) ("All applicants and registrants shall provide effective controls to guard against theft and diversion of controlled substances ...").

[11] 21 U.S.C. §812(b)(1).

[12] Very narrow exceptions to the federal prohibition do exist. For example, one may legally use marijuana if participating in an FDA approved study or participate in the Compassionate Investigational New Drug program.

[13] 21 U.S.C. §844(a).

[14] 21 U.S.C. §841(b).

[15] Ogden Memorandum, *supra* note 5.

[16] *Id.* at 1-2.

[17] *Id.* at 3.

[18] Memorandum for U.S. Attorneys from James M. Cole, Deputy Attorney General, *Guidance Regarding the Ogden Memo in Jurisdictions Seeking to Authorize Marijuana for Medical Use*, October 19, 2009 (hereinafter Cole Memorandum).

[19] *Id.* at 2.

[20] William Yardley, *New Federal Crackdown Confounds States that Allow Medical Marijuana*, N.Y. Times (May 7, 2011).

[21] *See*, Chad Livengood and Doug Denison, *Medical Marijuana Law Busted*, The News Journal (Delaware), February 12, 2012; Olivia Katrandjian, *Under Federal Threat, Washington Governor Vetoes Medical Marijuana Dispensary Bill*, ABC News, April 30, 2011.

[22] On November 6, 2012, Colorado and Washington became the first states to decriminalize marijuana for recreational use. *See*, Colorado Ballot Initiative Amendment 64, *available at*: http://www.sos.state.co.us/pubs/elections/Initiatives/ titleBoard/filings/2011-2012/ 30Final.pdf; Washington Ballot Initiative I-502, *available at*: http://sos.wa.gov/_assets/elections/initiatives/i502.pdf. The approved ballot initiatives legalize the possession of small amounts of marijuana and regulate and tax the drug as the state does other substances such as alcohol and tobacco. A legal analysis of these recently adopted laws is beyond the scope of this report; however, for a brief discussion of the legal issues that arise as a result of these measures, see CRS Legal Sidebar WSLG295, Can a State Really "Legalize" Marijuana, by Todd Garvey. In addition, some states and localities treat the possession of small amounts of marijuana (typically one ounce or less) as a civil, rather than criminal, offense. *See, e.g.*, Colo. Rev. Stat. §18-18-406 ("any person who possesses two ounces or less of marijuana commits a class 2 petty offense … punished by a fine of not more than one hundred dollars.").

[23] State exemptions often apply not only to the patients, but also primary caregivers and physicians. *See, e.g.*, Nev. Rev. Stat. §453A.220.

[24] For purposes of this report, the term "state" includes the District of Columbia.

[25] *See, e.g.*, R.I. Gen Laws §21-28.6-4.

[26] California permits an "oral recommendation." Cal. Health & Safety Code §11362.5.

[27] *See, e.g.*, Wash. Rev. Code §69.51A.040.

[28] *See, e.g.*, Colo. Const. Art. XVIII §14.

[29] *See. e.g.*, Ore. Rev. Stat. §§475.316, 475.319.
[30] *See, e.g.*, Ariz. Rev. Stat. §36-2806.02.
[31] Cal. Health & Safety Code §11362.765.
[32] *See*, Robert A. Mikos, *On the Limits of Supremacy: Medical Marijuana and the States' Overlooked Power to Legalize Federal Crime*, 62 Vand. L. Rev. 1421, 1432 (2009) ("Most states, however have simply refused or neglected to address the issue ... This means that qualified patients must often resort to the black market to obtain the marijuana they are legally entitled to possess.").
[33] 545 U.S. 1 (2005).
[34] *Id.* at 15.
[35] *Id.* at 17-18 ("The similarities between this case and *Wickard* are striking."). In Wickard v. Filburn, 317 U.S. 111 (1942), the Court held that the Agricultural Adjustment Act's federal quota system applied to bushels of wheat that were homegrown and personally consumed.
[36] *Raich*, 545 U.S. at 19.
[37] *Id.* ("[T]he diversion of homegrown marijuana tends to frustrate the federal interest in eliminating commercial transactions in the interstate market in their entirety.").
[38] *Id.* at 22.
[39] *Id.* at 29.
[40] U.S. Const. amend. X ("The powers not delegated to the United States by the Constitution, nor prohibited by it to the States, are reserved to the States respectively, or to the people.").
[41] National League of Cities v. Usery, 426 U.S. 833 (1976).
[42] New York v. United States, 505 U.S. 144 (1992).
[43] *Id.*
[44] *Id.* at 175.
[45] 521 U.S. 898 (1997).
[46] *Id.* at 904-918.
[47] In *Reno v. Condon*, the Supreme Court held that a federal law does not "commandeer" state resources so long as it "does not require the States in their sovereign capacities to regulate their own citizens," but rather regulates state activities directly. 528 U.S. 141, 151 (2000).
[48] *See*, South Dakota v. Dole, 483 U.S. 203 (1987); *New York*, 505 U.S. at 188 (pointing out that the Spending Clause provides an alternative to the congressional "commandeering" of state officials that violated the Tenth Amendment).
[49] See, Printz v. United States, 521 U.S. 898, 933, 138 L. Ed. 2d 914, 117 S. Ct. 2365 (1997) (O'Connor, J., concurring) (discussing ability of state officials to voluntarily continue to participate in a federal program).
[50] *See, e.g.*, Wickard v. Filburn, 317 U.S. 111, 124 (1942)("[N]o form of state activity can constitutionally thwart the regulatory power granted by the commerce clause to Congress").
[51] 21 U.S.C. §903 (limiting the preemptive scope of the CSA to only those state laws that create a "positive conflict" with federal law).
[52] U.S. Const., Art. VI, cl. 2.
[53] Northern States Power Co. v. Minnesota, 447 F.2d 1143, 1145 (8th Cir. 1971).
[54] Rice v. Santa Fe Elevator Corp., 331 U.S. 218, 230 (1947).
[55] Hines v. Davidowitz, 312 U.S. 52, 67 (1941); *See also*, English v. General Elec. Co., 496 U.S. 72, 79 (1990) ("By referring to these three categories, we should not be taken to mean that they are rigidly distinct.").
[56] Skull Valley Band of Goshute Indians v. Nielson, 376 F.3d 1223, 1240 (10th Cir. 2004) (citing Wardair Canada, Inc. v. Florida Dep't of Revenue 477 U.S. 1 (1986)).
[57] *See, e.g.*, Norfolk & Western Ry. v. American Train Dispatchers' Ass'n, 499 U.S. 117 (1991).
[58] However, where Congress legislates in an area displacing "the historic police powers of the States," courts should imply preemption only where it is the "clear and manifest purpose of Congress." Rice v. Santa Fe Elevator Corp., 331 U.S. 218, 230 (1947).
[59] *See*, Gade v. National Solid Waste Management Assn., 505 U.S. 88, 98 (1992).
[60] *Santa Fe Elevator Corp.*, 331 U.S. at 230 (1947).

[61] 21 U.S.C. §903 (emphasis added).

[62] *Id.*

[63] *See, e.g.*, Emerald Steel Fabricators, Inc., v. Bureau of Labor and Industries, 348 Ore. 159 (2010); *But see*, County of San Diego v. San Diego Norml, 165 Cal. App. 4th 798 (2008)(holding that a state law conflicts with the CSA only where it is impossible to comply with both the state and federal law.).

[64] *See*, Wyeth v. Levine, 555 U.S. 555 (2009); Barnett Bank v. Nelson, 517 U.S. 25 (1996).

[65] *Barnett Bank*, 517 U.S. at 31. (holding that a federal statute that permitted national banks to sell insurance and a state statute that prohibited banks from selling insurance did not "impose directly conflicting duties").

[66] Freightliner Corp. v. Myrick, 514 U.S. 280, 287 (1947).

[67] Crosby v. National Foreign Trade Council, 530 U.S. 363, 373 (2000)(In considering obstacle preemption, a court's judgment is to be informed by "examining the federal statute as a whole and identifying its purpose and intended effects.").

[68] *Id.*

[69] Rice v. Santa Fe Elevator Corp., 331 U.S. 218 (1947).

[70] County of San Diego v. San Diego Norml, 165 Cal. App. 4th 798 (2008) (citing Boyle v. United Technologies Corp., 487 U.S. 500, 507 (1988)).

[71] *See, e.g.*, United States v. Oakland Cannabis Buyers' Cooperative, 532 U.S. 483 (2001)(holding that there is no medical necessity defense under the CSA, even where state law recognizes such a defense.) United States v. Stacy, 734 F. Supp. 2d 1074 (S.D. Cal. 2010); United States v. Lynch, 2010 U.S. Dist. LEXIS 53011(C.D. Cal. 2010).

[72] *Stacy*, 734 F. Supp. at 1079 ("[T[he fact that an individual may not be prosecuted under [state] law does not provide him or her with immunity under federal law."); United states v. Rosenthal, 454 F.3d 943 (9th Cir. 2006) (holding that state medical marijuana law could not act as a shield to federal prosecution.)

[73] *Stacy*, 734 F. Supp. at 1084.

[74] *See, Crosby*, 530 U.S. at 373.

[75] Qualified Patients Assoc. v. City of Anaheim, 187 Cal. App. 4th 734 (2010) (citing Conant v. Walters, 309 F.3d 629, 646 (9th Cir. 2002) (Kozinski, J. concurring) ("That patients may be more likely to violate federal law if the additional deterrent of state liability is removed may worry the federal government, but the proper response—according to *New York* and *Printz*—is to ratchet up the federal regulatory regime, *not* to commandeer that of the state.").

[76] Cal. Health & Safety Code §11362.5.

[77] *Id.*

[78] People v. Kelly, 222 P.3d 186 (Cal. 2010).

[79] Cal. Health & Safety Code §11362.765.

[80] *See*, Assenberg, et al. v. Anacortes Housing Authority, 2006 U.S. Dist. LEXIS 34002 (W.D. Wash. 2006)("[T]o the extent that the state law legalizes marijuana use and prohibits the forfeiture of public housing, it conflicts with the CSA and the federal statutes and regulations that criminalize marijuana use and prohibit illegal drug use in public housing.").

[81] *Mikos*, *supra* note 32 at 1457-59 ("A handful of states have proposed supplying marijuana directly to qualified patients via state-operated farms and distribution centers ... The CSA, however, clearly preempts any such state program.). Professor Mikos notes that both Maine and New Mexico have "seriously considered supplying marijuana directly to qualified patients through state-run distribution centers." *Id.* at 1432.

[82] State courts in states with medical marijuana laws have been at the forefront of marijuana preemption litigation. Some of these cases arise as a result of localities challenging state medical marijuana laws—and the obligations those laws place on the localities—as preempted under the CSA. *See, e.g.*, City of Riverside v. Inland Empire Patient's Health and Wellness Center, Inc., 200 Cal. App. 4th 885 (2011), review granted, 2012 Cal. LEXIS 1028 (Cal. January 18, 2012).

[83] Cal. Health & Safety Code §11362.71; Ore. Rev. Stat. §475.306.
[84] 165 Cal. App. 4th 798 (2008), review denied 2008 Cal. LEXIS 12220 (Cal. 2008).
[85] *Id.* at 808-809.
[86] *Id.* at 819 ("Congress intended to reject express and field preemption of state laws concerning controlled substances.").
[87] *Id.* at 823.
[88] *Id.* at 826-28.
[89] *Id.* at 825.
[90] *Id.* at 827. In what may be interpreted as a limiting paragraph, the court also noted that "[a]lthough California's decision to enact statutory exemptions from state criminal prosecution for such persons arguably undermines the goals or is inconsistent with the CSA—a question we do not decide here—any alleged 'obstacle' to the federal goals is presented by those California statutes that create the exemptions, not by the statutes providing a system for rapidly identifying exempt individuals.").
[91] 348 Ore. 159 (2010).
[92] *Id.* at 525.
[93] *Id.* at 520-22.
[94] O.R.S. §659A.112.
[95] *Emerald Steel*, 348 Ore. at 521.
[96] *Id.* at 526.
[97] *Id.* at 527-28.
[98] *Id.* at 528 ("To be sure, the two laws are logically inconsistent; state law authorizes what federal law prohibits. However, a person can comply with both laws by refraining from any use of marijuana …").
[99] *Id.* at 529.
[100] *Id.* at 530 ("[T]he validity of the exemptions and the validity of the authorization turn on different constitutional principles.").
[101] *Id.*
[102] Additionally, how important is the fact that *Emerald Steel* arose in an employment discrimination dispute? Would the Court have reached the same conclusion if the case arose in a different context?
[103] *See, e.g.*, 21 U.S.C. §846 (making it illegal to conspire to violate the CSA); 18 U.S.C. §§2-4, 371.
[104] *See, e.g.*, Ore. Rev. Stat. §475.323.
[105] 21 U.S.C. §885(d).
[106] *See*, State v. Karma, 39 P.3d 866 (Or. App. 2002)(finding immunity for city police). If a state officer is acting pursuant to a preempted state medical marijuana provision, it is an open question as to whether he be "lawfully engaged in the enforcement of any law …"
[107] Letter from Jenny A. Durkan, U.S. Attorney for the Western District of Washington and Michael C. Ormsby, U.S. Attorney for the Eastern District of Washington, to the Honorable Christine Gregoire, Washington State Governor, April 14, 2011.
[108] *Id.*
[109] Arizona v. United States, Case No. CV 11-1072-PHX-SRB (D.C. Ariz. January 4, 2012) at 3. Governors of five other states have reportedly received similar letters. William Yardley, *New Federal Crackdown Confounds States that Allow Medical Marijuana*, N.Y. Times (May 7, 2011).
[110] Arizona v. United States, Case No. CV 11-1072-PHX-SRB (D.C. Ariz. January 4, 2012) at 7.
[111] *Id.* at 8.
[112] Ogden Memorandum, *supra* note 5 at 1-2.
[113] United States v. Goodwin, 457 U.S. 368, 380 (1982).
[114] Wayte v. United States, 470 U.S. 598, 607 (1985).
[115] United States v. Batchelder, 442 U.S. 114, 125 (1979).
[116] Oyler v. Boles, 368 U.S. 448, 456 (1962).

[117] *Batchelder*, 442 U.S. at 124 ("Whether to prosecute … [is a] decision[] that generally rest[s] in the prosecutor's discretion.").

[118] The President has the constitutional obligation to "take care that the laws be faithfully executed." U.S. Const. Art II, §3. Moreover, although the effect of the provision is debated, 28 U.S.C. §547 directs that "except as otherwise provided by law, each United States attorney, within his district, shall—prosecute for all offenses against the United States …"

In: Recreational and Medical Marijuana
Editors: Valentin Dijkstra
ISBN: 978-1-62808-114-5

Chapter 3

THE CONTROLLED SUBSTANCES ACT: REGULATORY REQUIREMENTS*

Brian T. Yeh

SUMMARY

This report highlights certain non-criminal regulatory requirements of the Controlled Substances Act (CSA). The CSA and its implementing regulations establish a framework through which the federal government regulates the use of controlled substances for legitimate medical, scientific, research, and industrial purposes, and prevents these substances from being diverted for illegal purposes. The CSA assigns various plants, drugs, and chemicals (such as narcotics, stimulants, depressants, hallucinogens, and anabolic steroids) to one of five schedules based on the substance's medical use, potential for abuse, and safety or dependence liability. Schedule I contains substances that have no currently accepted medical use and cannot safely be made available to the public under a prescription, while Schedules II, III, IV, and V include substances that have recognized medical uses and may be manufactured, distributed, and used in accordance with the CSA. The order of the schedules reflects substances that are progressively less dangerous and addictive. To

* This is an edited, reformatted and augmented version of the Congressional Research Service Publication, CRS Report for Congress RL34635, dated December 13, 2012.

restrict access to chemicals used in the illicit manufacture of certain controlled substances, the CSA also regulates 40 "listed chemicals." Furthermore, the CSA regulates controlled substance "analogues," which are substances that are not controlled but are structurally or pharmacologically similar to substances found in Schedule I or II and have no accepted medical use.

Unless specifically exempted by the CSA, any person who handles controlled substances or listed chemicals (such as drug manufacturers, wholesale distributors, doctors, hospitals, pharmacies, and scientific researchers) must register with the Drug Enforcement Administration (DEA) in the U.S. Department of Justice, which administers and enforces the CSA. Registrants must keep accurate and complete records of all transactions involving controlled substances, maintain detailed inventories of the substances in their possession, and periodically file reports with the DEA, as well as ensure that controlled substances are securely stored and safeguarded in accordance with DEA regulations.

Between 10%-11% of all drug prescriptions written in the United States are for pharmaceutical controlled substances. Only licensed medical practitioners (who are registered with the DEA) are authorized to prescribe controlled substances listed in Schedules II-V to patients; such prescriptions may only be issued by a practitioner who is "acting in the usual course of his professional practice," and for a "legitimate medical purpose." The CSA authorizes the DEA Administrator to suspend or revoke a physician's prescription privileges upon a finding that he has "committed such acts as would render his registration ... inconsistent with the public interest."

While the CSA provides criminal sanctions for *illicit* possession, manufacture, or distribution of controlled substances, the statute also contains a few noteworthy penalty provisions that are specifically applicable to persons who are authorized by the DEA to handle controlled substances lawfully. The CSA sets forth certain offenses involving listed chemicals and DEA registration and other prohibited acts relating to registrants who manufacture, distribute, and dispense controlled substances.

The Controlled Substances Act (CSA or the act)[1] is the statutory framework through which the federal government regulates the lawful production, possession, and distribution of controlled substances. The CSA places various plants, drugs, and chemicals (such as narcotics, stimulants, depressants, hallucinogens, and anabolic steroids) into one of five schedules based on the substance's medical use, potential for abuse, and safety or dependence liability. Further, the act requires persons who handle controlled substances or listed chemicals (such as drug manufacturers, wholesale distributors, doctors, hospitals, pharmacies, and scientific researchers) to register with the Drug Enforcement Administration (DEA) in the U.S. Department of Justice, which administers and enforces the CSA. Registrants must maintain detailed records of their respective controlled substance inventories as well as establish adequate security controls to minimize theft and diversion.[2] Although the CSA sets forth criminal provisions[3] for the unlawful manufacture, possession, and distribution of controlled substances, this report will instead focus on the act's non-criminal regulatory requirements[4] for those who legitimately produce, distribute, and dispense controlled substances.

FORMAL SCHEDULING

The placement of drugs or other substances into schedules under the CSA is based upon the substance's medical use, potential for abuse, and safety or dependence liability.[5] The act further provides a mechanism for substances to be controlled,[6] or added to a schedule; decontrolled, or removed from the scheduling framework altogether; and rescheduled or transferred from one schedule to another.[7]

The proceedings to add, delete, or change the schedule of a drug or substance may be initiated by the DEA, the U.S. Department of Health and Human Services (HHS), or by petition by any interested person.[8] When a petition is received by the DEA, the agency initiates its own investigation of the drug or substance. The DEA may also initiate an investigation at any time in response to information received from law enforcement laboratories, state and local law enforcement and regulatory agencies, or other sources of information.

After the DEA's initial investigation, the DEA Administrator (Administrator)[9] requests from the Assistant Secretary of Health of HHS (Assistant Secretary of Health) a scientific and medical evaluation and recommendation as to whether the drug or substance should be controlled or removed from control.[10] The Assistant Secretary of Health in turn solicits information from the Commissioner of the Food and Drug Administration, and obtains evaluations and recommendations from the National Institute on Drug Abuse. The Assistant Secretary of Health then consolidates the requested information and transmits back to the DEA a medical and scientific evaluation regarding the drug or substance, along with a recommendation as to whether the drug or substance should be controlled and into which schedule it should be placed.[11]

The Administrator then evaluates all of the relevant data and makes a final determination as to whether the drug or substance should be controlled or removed entirely from control.[12] In making a determination regarding the control of a drug or substance, the Administrator must consider factors such as the drug's actual or relative potential for abuse; scientific evidence of its pharmacological effect; the current state of scientific knowledge regarding the drug or substance; the risk to the public health; and whether the substance is an immediate precursor of a substance already controlled under the act.[13] After the Administrator makes such a determination, he must make specific findings concerning the drug or substance that dictate the schedule in which the drug or substance will be placed.[14]

Congress may also add a substance to a schedule through legislation.

Emergency or Temporary Scheduling

The CSA was amended by the Comprehensive Crime Control Act of 1984[15] to include a provision allowing the Administrator to place a drug or substance, on a temporary basis, into Schedule I when necessary to avoid an "imminent hazard to public safety."[16] The Administrator, however, may not issue a temporary scheduling order until thirty days after he notifies both the public and the HHS Secretary of his intent to issue the temporary scheduling order and of his justification for issuing the order.[17] Further, the Administrator must consider any of the HHS Secretary's comments regarding the temporary order.[18]

When issuing a temporary scheduling order, the Administrator must consider, with respect to the finding of an imminent hazard to public safety (i) the history of the drug or substance and its current pattern of abuse; (ii) the scope, duration, and significance of the drug or substance's abuse; (iii) the risk to public health; (iv) diversion of the drug or substance from legitimate channels; and (v) the drug or substance's "clandestine importation, manufacture, or distribution."[19] A drug or substance may be temporarily scheduled for two years and possibly longer—up to an additional year—if formal scheduling procedures have been initiated.[20] This emergency scheduling applies only to substances with no accepted medical use in the United States.

Listed Chemicals

In an effort to restrict access to chemicals used in the illicit manufacture of certain controlled substances in violation of the CSA, Congress passed the Chemical Diversion and Trafficking Act (CDTA) in 1988.[21] The CDTA and its subsequent amendments[22] allow the DEA to control 40 chemicals[23] and restrict their diversion. These 40 chemicals are referred to by the CSA as "listed chemicals."[24] Listed chemicals are divided into two categories: List I[25] and List II.[26] While both categories of chemicals can be used to illicitly manufacture controlled substances, List I chemicals are more strenuously regulated than List II chemicals because List I chemicals are "important to the manufacture of a controlled substance."[27]

Controlled Substances Analogues

Controlled substance analogues are substances that are not controlled but are structurally or pharmacologically similar to substances found in Schedule I or II and have no accepted medical use.[28] A substance that meets the definition of the term "controlled substance analogue" and is intended for human consumption is treated as if it were a controlled substance in Schedule I.[29] Controlled substance analogues are different from listed chemicals because such analogues are typically intended for human consumption as a substitute for a controlled substance, whereas listed chemicals are not intended for human consumption but are instead used as "ingredients" in the manufacture of certain controlled substances.

Synthetic Drugs

Synthetic drugs are chemically produced in a laboratory; their chemical structure can be either identical to or different from naturally occurring drugs, and their effects are designed to mimic or even enhance those of natural drugs.[30] Many synthetic cathinones (central nervous system stimulants) are marketed under household names such as "bath salts" or "plant food" and are stamped with the warning "not intended for human consumption." This action is intended to circumvent the CSA's statutory definition of a controlled substance analogue. In October 2011, the DEA used its temporary scheduling authority to place three synthetic cathinones on Schedule I of the CSA.[31] In June 2012, Congress passed the Synthetic Drug Abuse Prevention Act of 2012—Subtitle D of Title XI of the Food and Drug Administration Safety and Innovation Act (P.L. 112-144)—which permanently added two of these synthetic cathinones to Schedule I of the CSA, along with cannabimimetic substances (commonly referred to as synthetic marijuana).[32]

International Treaty Obligations

The United States is a party to the Single Convention on Narcotic Drugs of 1961, which was designed to establish effective control over international and domestic traffic in narcotics, coca leaf, cocaine, and marijuana. The United States is also party to the Convention on Psychotropic Substances of 1971, which was designed to establish similar control over stimulants, depressants, and hallucinogens. Treaty obligations may require the Attorney General to control or reschedule a substance if existing controls are less stringent than those required by a treaty.[33]

REGULATION

The CSA creates a "closed system" of distribution[34] in which distribution may lawfully occur among registered handlers of controlled substances, referred to as "registrants."[35] Central to this closed system of distribution is the registration of all persons or entities authorized by the DEA to handle controlled substances. The DEA has described the movement of a controlled substance from manufacture to the patient as follows:

> [A] controlled substance, after being manufactured by a DEA-registered manufacturer, may be transferred to a DEA-registered distributor for subsequent distribution to a DEA- registered retail pharmacy. After a DEA-registered practitioner, such as a physician or a dentist, issues a prescription for a controlled substance to a patient (i.e., the ultimate user), that patient can fill that prescription at a retail pharmacy to obtain that controlled substance. In this system, the manufacturer, the distributor, the practitioner, and the retail pharmacy are all required to be DEA registrants, or to be exempted from the requirement of registration, to participate in the process.[36]

All registrants are required by the CSA to maintain complete and accurate inventories and records of all regulated transactions involving controlled substances and listed chemicals, as well as provide adequate security controls to prevent their diversion. Therefore, a particular controlled substance is always under the control of a DEA-registered person until it reaches the patient or is destroyed, and the CSA's regulatory requirements "ensure that all controlled substances are accounted for from their creation until their dispensing or destruction."[37]

Registration

The CSA defines who must register with the DEA in order to handle controlled substances.[38] Every person who manufactures, distributes, dispenses, imports, or exports any controlled substance, or who proposes to engage in the manufacture, distribution, dispensing, importation, or exportation of any controlled substance, must register with the DEA, unless they are exempt.[39] Generally, all manufacturers, distributors, and practitioners who deal with controlled substances must register. The CSA refers to an individual patient as an "ultimate user," which it defines as "a person who has lawfully obtained, and who possesses, a controlled substance for his own use or for the use of a member of his household or for an animal owned by him or by a member of his household."[40] Ultimate users are not required to register with the DEA[41] because the controlled substances in their possession "are no longer part of the closed system of distribution and are no longer subject to DEA's system of corresponding accountability."[42]

Manufacturers and distributors of controlled substances must register with the DEA annually, and those who dispense controlled substances must obtain registrations that may not be issued for less than one year or more than three years.[43] Any person who is required to register in order to manufacture, distribute, or dispense controlled substances, but has not yet registered, may apply for registration at any time.[44] Those who already are registered can apply for re-registration not more than 60 days before the expiration date of their current registration.[45] Registrations specify the extent to which registrants are authorized to manufacture, possess, distribute, or dispense controlled substances. The Administrator is authorized to charge reasonable fees relating to the registration and control of the manufacturing, distribution, and dispensing of controlled substances under the act.[46] In addition, the

Administrator can inspect the establishments of registrants or applicants for registration.[47]

Registration is granted to applicants only if it would be consistent with the "public interest" to do so.[48] The Administrator uses several criteria to assess whether registering an applicant is consistent with the "public interest." The criteria differ depending on the substance involved and whether the applicant is a manufacturer, distributor, or practitioner, but generally include factors such as those relating to public health and safety and compliance with state and local laws.[49]

The Administrator also has the authority to deny, revoke, or suspend registrations under certain circumstances but must provide adequate grounds for doing so.[50] Before the DEA can deny an application, the agency must provide the applicant with an opportunity to demonstrate why the registration should not be denied.[51] However, the Administrator can suspend without notice any registration in order to avoid imminent danger to public health and safety.[52] A revocation or suspension of a registration may be applicable to a particular controlled substance or class of controlled substances. For example, a manufacturer who has been found to have violated the registration provisions regarding a Schedule II substance will still be able to manufacture controlled substances in Schedules III-V because the revocation or suspension relates only to one class of controlled substances.[53]

The registration of an individual terminates when the person dies, ceases legal existence, or discontinues business or professional practice.[54] A registrant who ceases legal existence or discontinues business or professional practice must notify the DEA promptly of this occurrence. A registration cannot be transferred to someone else unless the Administrator provides his express, written consent for such a transfer to occur.[55]

In some instances, applicants must apply for several separate registrations in order to comply with the CSA. Separate registrations are required for each principal place of business or professional practice where controlled substances are manufactured, distributed, imported, exported, or dispensed.[56] For example, a physician who is regularly engaged in dispensing controlled substances at one location must register to dispense controlled substances at other locations if he chooses to dispense controlled substances at these other locations.[57] However, with the enactment of the Ryan Haight Online Pharmacy Consumer Protection Act of 2008, the DEA Administrator must modify existing registrations of pharmacies to authorize them to dispense controlled substances by means of the Internet, unless the Administrator determines that such modification would be inconsistent with the public interest.[58]

Recordkeeping Requirements

In addition to registration requirements, the CSA contains several recordkeeping provisions.[59] A registrant authorized to handle controlled substances must keep accurate records and maintain detailed inventories in compliance with applicable federal and state law. For example, a registrant must maintain a complete and accurate record of each substance manufactured, received, sold, delivered, or otherwise disposed of by the registrant.[60] Furthermore, inventories must be available for inspection for at least two years.[61] These records are generally open for inspection by federal authorities and state officers tasked with enforcing state narcotics laws.[62] The CSA declares that is unlawful for any person to "refuse or negligently fail to make, keep, or furnish any record, report, notification, declaration, order or order form, statement, invoice, or information required" by the CSA;[63] it is also unlawful for any person knowingly or intentionally "to furnish false or fraudulent material information in, or omit any material information from, any application, report, record, or other document required to be made, kept, or filed" under the CSA.[64]

Certain DEA regulations implementing the CSA also apply to listed chemicals.[65] For example, all registrants authorized to handle listed chemicals (List I and List II) must maintain records of regulated transactions and submit various reports to the DEA.[66] However, the Administrator has the authority to exempt specified concentrations of listed chemical mixtures from the recordkeeping requirements set forth in section 830 of the act that require registrants to maintain detailed records of every regulated transaction.[67]

Distribution

As a means to ensure that only authorized registrants obtain Schedule I and II drugs from manufacturers and distributors, the CSA requires registrants who legitimately distribute[68] controlled substances or listed chemicals to keep records of shipments to purchasers.[69] Manufacturers and distributors must receive a special order form from a purchaser prior to shipping Schedule I and II drugs.[70] The form is preprinted by the DEA with the name and address of the purchaser and the drugs must be shipped by the supplier filling the order to the purchaser's registered location.[71] All manufacturers must forward copies of completed order forms to the DEA by the close of the month in which the shipment is made.[72] The CSA also provides for electronic orders of Schedule I and II drugs.[73] Manufacturers must also forward copies of filled electronic orders to the DEA within 2 business days.[74]

The DEA further monitors the distribution of controlled substances by requiring manufacturers and distributors of Schedule I and II drugs to file reports[75] through the Automated Reports and Consolidated Orders System (ARCOS).[76] Certain narcotics listed in Schedules III and IV are also covered by the ARCOS reporting requirements.[77]

Registered pharmacies that are authorized to dispense controlled substances by means of the Internet must report to the DEA Administrator the total quantity of each controlled substance that the pharmacy has dispensed each month.[78] In addition, online pharmacies[79] must clearly display on their website homepage a statement that they comply with federal and state law concerning the delivery or sale of controlled substances, as well as post certain disclosure information such as

- the name and address of the pharmacy as it appears on the pharmacy's DEA registration certificate,
- the pharmacy's telephone number and email address,
- a list of states in which the pharmacy is licensed to dispense controlled substance,
- the identification and contact information of the pharmacist-in-charge, and
- the following statement: "This online pharmacy will only dispense a controlled substance to a person who has a valid prescription issued for a legitimate medical purpose based upon a medical relationship with a prescribing practitioner. This includes at least one prior in-person medical evaluation or medical evaluation via telemedicine in accordance with applicable requirements of section 309."[80]

An online pharmacy must notify the DEA Administrator, and the state boards of pharmacy in any states in which the online pharmacies operate, thirty days before offering a controlled substance for sale, delivery, distribution, or dispensing; such notification must include pharmacy's Internet site address, the information that is required to be posted on the pharmacy's website, and the DEA registration numbers of the pharmacy and practitioners who work for it.[81] Online pharmacies that were already operational as of April 13, 2009, had to submit this notification to the DEA Administrator and any applicable state boards of pharmacy no later than May 12, 2009.

Dispensing to Patients

The CSA further provides special control mechanisms for licensed practitioners and pharmacists who dispense[82] controlled substances in Schedules II-V to patients for legitimate medical purposes. Because controlled substances classified as Schedule I drugs are deemed to have no accepted medical purpose in the United States, they may only be used for research, and practitioners may not prescribe them to patients. Under the CSA, only licensed medical practitioners[83] are authorized to prescribe controlled substances listed in Schedules II-V to patients.[84] A prescription for a controlled substance must be "issued for a legitimate medical purpose by an individual practitioner acting in the usual course of his professional practice."[85] Accordingly, practitioners have a responsibility to ensure that the controlled substance is properly prescribed and dispensed.[86]

No controlled substance in Schedules II may be dispensed to a patient by a pharmacist without a written prescription[87] from a practitioner, except in certain cases where the practitioner administers the controlled substance directly to the patient.[88] However, in the case of an emergency situation, a practitioner may orally authorize a pharmacist to fill a prescription for a Schedule II controlled substance. DEA regulations define "emergency situation" as those in which the prescribing practitioner determines:[89]

1. that immediate administration of the controlled substance is necessary, for proper treatment of the intended ultimate user; and
2. that no appropriate alternative treatment is available, including administration of a drug which is not a controlled substance under schedule II of the act; and
3. that it is not reasonably possible for the prescribing practitioner to provide a written prescription to be presented to the person dispensing the substance, prior to the dispensing.

Such an emergency oral authorization for a Schedule II substance may be filled by a pharmacist if the following conditions are met:[90]

1. the quantity of the drug prescribed and dispensed is limited to an amount adequate to treat the patient during the emergency period;
2. the prescription is immediately reduced to writing by the pharmacist and contains all the information that federal regulations require of

prescriptions,[91] except for the signature of the prescribing individual practitioner;
3. if the prescribing individual practitioner is not known to the pharmacist, he must make a reasonable effort to determine that the oral authorization came from a registered individual practitioner, which may include a callback to the prescribing individual practitioner using his phone number as listed in the telephone directory and/or other good faith efforts to insure his identity; and
4. within seven days after authorizing an emergency oral prescription, the prescribing individual practitioner must deliver a written prescription to the dispensing pharmacist. The practitioner must write on the face of the prescription "Authorization for Emergency Dispensing" and also write the date of the oral order. Upon receipt, the dispensing pharmacist must attach this paper prescription to the oral emergency prescription that had earlier been reduced to writing. The pharmacist must notify the nearest DEA office if the prescribing individual practitioner fails to deliver a written prescription to him; failure of the pharmacist to do so shall void the authority to dispense without a written prescription of a prescribing individual practitioner.

Controlled substances in Schedules III-V may be dispensed by a pharmacy pursuant to either a written or oral prescription, including a facsimile of a written prescription;[92] these substances may also be administered or dispensed directly by the practitioner in the course of his professional practice without a prescription.[93]

Practitioners are permitted to sign and transmit electronic prescriptions for controlled substances, assuming that the electronic prescription complies with detailed requirements set forth in the applicable federal regulations.[94]

Pharmacists may partially fill a prescription for Schedule II substances under certain circumstances.[95] Pharmacists are prohibited from refilling prescriptions for Schedule II substances.[96] Prescriptions for controlled substances in Schedules III and IV, however, may be filled or refilled by pharmacists up to five times within six months after the date on which the prescription was issued, unless the prescribing practitioner authorizes a renewal of the prescription.[97] A pharmacy may process electronic prescriptions for controlled substances if it has satisfied several conditions described in the applicable federal regulations.[98]

A controlled substance that is a prescription drug may not be delivered, distributed, or dispensed by means of the Internet without a "valid prescription."[99] Only with respect to this provision of the Controlled Substances Act, a "valid prescription" means a prescription that is issued for a legitimate medical purpose in the usual course of professional practice by a practitioner who has conducted at least one medical evaluation of the patient in the physical presence of the practitioner.[100]

Quotas

The DEA limits the quantity of Schedule I and II controlled substances which may be produced in a given calendar year. The CSA authorizes the Administrator to

- establish aggregate production quotas for all manufacturers;
- establish individual production quotas for specific registered manufactures;
- establish individual production quotas for registrants who have not manufactured controlled substances during one or more proceeding years; and
- implement quota increases for individual manufacturers where necessary.[101]

By regulation, the Administrator must consider the following factors in making his quota determinations: (i) the total disposal of the controlled substance during the current and two preceding years; (ii) trends in the national rate of new disposal of the controlled substance; (iii) total inventories (actual or estimated) of "the class and all substances manufactured from the class [of controlled substances listed in Schedule I or II];" (iv) projected demand for a particular controlled substance; and (v) other relevant factors affecting the use of controlled substances including, changes in the currently accepted medical use of a controlled substance, the economic and physical availability of the raw materials necessary to produce a controlled substance, and recent unforeseen emergencies (i.e., natural disasters).[102]

Security

For the purposes of ensuring the secure storage and distribution of controlled substances and listed chemicals, all applicants and registrants must generally "provide effective controls and procedures to guard against theft and diversion of controlled substances."[103] DEA regulations further require all applicants and registrants to substantially comply with specific security standards for storage of controlled substances and List I chemicals.[104] Applicants and registrants must also be prepared to make adjustments to their security systems in the event that a controlled substance is transferred to another schedule or removed from control under the CSA.[105]

DEA regulations also detail specific security requirements for the different types of applicants and registrants. For example, non-practitioners (i.e., manufacturers, distributors, and narcotic treatment programs) are required to store Schedule I and II substances in electronically monitored safes, steel cabinets or vaults that meet or exceed certain specifications.[106] Licensed practitioners must store controlled substances in a "securely locked, substantially constructed cabinet"[107] and must notify the DEA of the theft or significant loss of any controlled substances within one business day of discovering such loss or theft.[108] Furthermore, all practitioners are prohibited from hiring employees who have been convicted of a drug-related felony or who have had a DEA registration denied or revoked.[109] DEA regulations recommend that non-practitioners carefully screen individuals before hiring them as employees, to ensure that job applicants do not have convictions for crimes or have engaged in unauthorized use of controlled substances.[110]

Disposal of Controlled Substances[111]

DEA registrants may need to dispose of controlled substances in their possession when they are expired, damaged, contaminated, or otherwise unwanted. Under the CSA and DEA regulations, there are three different options for registrants to dispose of controlled substances:[112]

1. The distributor or dispenser may return the controlled substance to the pharmaceutical manufacturer who accepts returns of outdated or damaged controlled substances.
2. The distributor, dispenser, or manufacturer may itself dispose of the controlled substances under procedures specified by federal regulation.[113]
3. The distributor, dispenser, or manufacturer may transfer the controlled substances to a "reverse distributor" to take custody of the controlled

substances for the purpose of returning them to the manufacturer or arranging for their disposal.[114]

Penalties

While the criminal provisions of the CSA focus mainly on the *illicit* possession, manufacture, and distribution of controlled substances,[115] there are a few noteworthy penalty provisions applicable to persons registered with the DEA. The CSA sets forth certain offenses involving listed chemicals,[116] DEA registration,[117] and other prohibited acts related to registrants who manufacture, distribute and dispense controlled substances.[118]

With respect to DEA registration generally, registrants authorized to distribute or dispense any controlled substance are prohibited from distributing, dispensing, or manufacturing controlled substances that are not authorized by a registrant's registration.[119] Registrants must maintain accurate records and furnish them when required to do so by law enforcement officials.[120] Registrants must also maintain a degree of transparency by allowing law enforcement officials access to their premises for inspections authorized by the CSA.[121] Failure to adhere to the registration requirements of the CSA may subject a registrant to civil fines, imprisonment, or both.[122]

The CSA also proscribes certain acts related to the manufacture and distribution of controlled substances and listed chemicals. Registrants who knowingly or intentionally (i) distribute Schedule I and II substances without a valid order form;[123] (ii) use an invalid registration number during the course of handling or acquiring controlled substances;[124] (iii) furnish false or fraudulent material information in a record or report required by the act;[125] or (iv) present false or fraudulent identification when receiving a listed chemical,[126] are subject to criminal fines, imprisonment, or both.[127] Additionally, registrants who violate the aforementioned provisions may be subject to injunctive or declarative actions filed by the Attorney General in federal district court.[128]

Finally, the CSA specifies several offenses regarding listed chemicals. For example, criminal fines and/or imprisonment are available for any person who knowingly or intentionally (i) possesses a listed chemical with the intent to manufacture a controlled substance without proper registration; (ii) possesses or distributes a listed chemical with knowledge or a reasonable belief that the listed chemical will be used to manufacture a controlled substance; or (iii) evades the CSA's recordkeeping and reporting requirements by receiving or distributing listed chemicals in small units.[129] Also, any person who knowingly possesses or distributes listed chemicals in violation of the CSA, or knowingly violates the CSA's recordkeeping requirements, is subject to criminal fines, imprisonment, or both.[130] Furthermore, in addition to the other applicable penalties, violators of the aforementioned provisions may also be enjoined for up to ten years from handling listed chemicals.[131]

EXCEPTIONS TO THE REGULATORY REQUIREMENTS UNDER THE CSA

It is important to note that the CSA allows for exceptions and also exempts certain individuals from some or all of its regulatory requirements. For example, individuals exempted from registration requirements include, among others, officers or employees of the DEA, officers of the U.S. Customs Service, offers or employees of the U.S. Food and Drug Administration, and any other federal officers who are authorized to possess, import, or export controlled substances in the course of their official duties.[132] Officers or employees of any state, or political subdivision of a state, who are engaged in enforcement of state or local laws relating to controlled substances, are also exempt from registering with the DEA.[133] A person who has lawfully obtained, and who possesses, a controlled substance for his own use is also not required to register.[134]

In addition, only those actually engaged in activities relating to manufacturing, distributing, and dispensing controlled substances are required to obtain registration, but related or affiliated persons who are not engaged in such activities are not required to register. For example, a stockholder or parent corporation of a corporation that manufactures controlled substances is not required to obtain registration, nor are employees of a registered manufacturer, distributor, or dispenser.[135]

The DEA Administrator may, by regulation, waive the registration requirement for certain manufacturers, distributors, or dispensers, if he finds it consistent with the public health and safety.[136]

In certain circumstances, the CSA recordkeeping provisions do not apply. The CSA recordkeeping provisions do not apply to the prescribing or administering of a controlled substance in Schedules II-V by practitioners acting in the lawful course of their professional practice *unless* such substance is prescribed or administered in the course of maintenance or detoxification treatment of an individual.[137] For example, the prescribing or administering of methadone for the treatment of narcotic addiction must be in conformity with the CSA's recordkeeping provisions. The CSA also does not apply to research conducted in conformity with the exemption granted under certain provisions of the Federal Food, Drug, and Cosmetic Act (FFDCA) or to preclinical research or teaching.[138]

APPENDIX. CLASSIFICATION OF CONTROLLED SUBSTANCES

Schedule	CSA Statutory Provision	Examples of Scheduled Substances
Schedule I	Pursuant to 21 U.S.C. § 812(b)(1), a substance will be placed in Schedule I based on specific findings made by the Administrator that "(A) The drug or other substance has a high potential for abuse. (B) The drug or other substance has no currently accepted medical use in treatment in the United States. (C) There is a lack of accepted safety for use of the drug or other substance under medical supervision."	Heroin, lysergic acid diethylamide (LSD), marijuana, MDMA (Ecstacy), methaqualone (Quaalude), synthetic marijuana.[a]
Schedule II	Pursuant to 21 U.S.C. § 812(b)(2), a substance will be placed in Schedule II based on specific findings made by the Administrator that "(A) The drug or substance has a high potential for abuse. (B) The drug or other substance has a currently accepted medical use in treatment in the United States or a currently accepted medical use with severe restrictions. (C) Abuse of the drug or other substance may lead to severe psychological or physical dependence."	Methadone, methamphetamine, methylphenidate (Ritalin®), morphine, oxycodone (OxyContin®), phencylidine (PCP).[b]
Schedule III	Pursuant to 21 U.S.C. § 812(b)(3), a substance will be placed in Schedule III based on specific findings made by the Administrator that "(A) The drug or other substance has a potential for abuse less than the drugs or other substances in schedules I and II. (B) The drug or other substance has a currently accepted medical use in treatment in the United States. (C) Abuse of the drug may lead to moderate or low physical dependence or high psychological dependence."	Anabolic steroids, synthetic delta—9 tetrahydrocannabinol (THC), codeine, hydrocodone with aspirin or Tylenol®.[c]
Schedule IV	Pursuant to 21 U.S.C. § 812(b)(4), a substance will be placed in Schedule IV based on specific findings made by the Administrator that "(A) The drug or other substance has a low potential for abuse relative to the drugs or other substances in schedule III. (B) The drug or other substance has a currently accepted medical use in treatment in the United States. (C) Abuse of the drug or other substance may lead to limited physical dependence or psychological dependence relative to the drugs or other substances in schedule III."	Xanax®, Valium®, Equanil®, Talwin®, Darvon®.[d]

(Continued)

Schedule	CSA Statutory Provision	Examples of Scheduled Substances
Schedule V	Pursuant to 21 U.S.C. § 812(b)(5), a substance will be placed in Schedule V based on specific findings made by the Administrator that "(A) The drug or other substance has a low potential for abuse relative to the drugs or other substances in schedule IV. (B) The drug or other substance has a currently accepted medical use in treatment in the United States. (C) Abuse of the drug or other substance may lead to limited physical dependence or psychological dependence relative to the drugs or other substances in schedule IV."	Certain cough medicines with codeine, and certain opium preparations.[e]

a. *See* 21 C.F.R. § 1308.11(b)-(f) (complete listing of Schedule I drugs and substances); *see also* 21 C.F.R. § 1308.11(g) (temporary listing of substances subject to emergency scheduling in Schedule I).
b. *See* 21 C.F.R. § 1308.12(b)-(g) (complete listing of Schedule II drugs and substances).
c. *See* 21 C.F.R. § 1308.13(b)-(g) (complete listing of Schedule III drugs and substances).
d. *See* 21 C.F.R. § 1308.14(b)-(f) (complete listing of Schedule IV drugs and substances).
e. *See* 21 C.F.R. § 1308.15(b)-(e) (complete listing of Schedule V drugs and substances).

End Notes

[1] 21 U.S.C. §§ 801 et seq.

[2] *See* 21 C.F.R. § 1304.11(a) ("Each inventory shall contain a complete and accurate record of all controlled substances on hand ..."); *see also* 21 C.F.R. § 1301.74(a) ("All applicants and registrants shall provide effective controls to guard against theft and diversion of controlled substances ...").

[3] For a detailed summary of the CSA's criminal provisions, *see* CRS Report RL30722, *Drug Offenses: Maximum Fines and Terms of Imprisonment for Violation of the Federal Controlled Substances Act and Related Laws*, by Brian T. Yeh.

[4] This report does not cover all the requirements under the CSA, nor does it address state controlled substances regulations. Although federal and state governments both regulate controlled substances, federal law preempts state law when state law conflicts with the CSA. 21 U.S.C. § 903.

[5] 21 U.S.C. §§ 811-812.

[6] For the purposes of the CSA, the term "control" as defined by 21 U.S.C. § 802(5) means "to add a drug or other substance, or immediate precursor, to a schedule under [§ 812 of the act], whether by transfer from another schedule or otherwise."

[7] The procedures for these actions are found at 21 U.S.C § 811.

[8] 21 U.S.C. § 811(a).

[9] Although the CSA grants to the Attorney General the authority to enforce its provisions, 21 U.S.C. §§ 801 et seq., the Attorney General has delegated this authority to the DEA Administrator at 28 C.F.R. § 0.100(b). Accordingly, the term "Administrator" will be used instead of the term "Attorney General" for the remainder of this report.

[10] 21 U.S.C. § 811(b).

[11] The medical and scientific evaluations are binding on the DEA with respect to such matters and form a part of the scheduling decision. The recommendation on the initial scheduling of a substance is binding only to the extent that if HHS recommends that the drug or substance not be controlled, the DEA may not add it to its schedules. *Id.*

[12] *Id.*

[13] *See* 21 U.S.C. § 811(c)(1)-(8) (complete listing of factors Administrator must consider when determining control or removal of substances from schedules).

[14] *See* 21 U.S.C. § 812(b) ("[A] drug or other substance may not be placed in any schedule unless the findings required for such schedule are made with respect to such drug or other substance"). For a summary of the findings necessary for Schedules I-V, *see* **Appendix**.

[15] P.L. 98-473.

[16] 21 U.S.C. § 811(h)(1).

[17] *Id.*

[18] 21 U.S.C. § 811(4).

[19] 21 U.S.C. § 811(h)(3).

[20] 21 U.S.C. § 811(h)(2), as amended by the Synthetic Drug Abuse Prevention Act of 2012, P.L. 112-144.

[21] P.L. 100-690.

[22] Domestic Chemical Diversion Control Act of 1993, P.L. 103-200; Comprehensive Methamphetamine Control Act of 1996, P.L. 104-237; Methamphetamine Anti-Proliferation Act of 2000, P.L. 106-310; Combat Methamphetamine Epidemic Act of 2005, P.L. 109-177.

[23] The 40 listed chemicals are set forth at 21 C.F.R. § 1310.02(a) and (b).

[24] *See* 21 U.S.C. §§ 802(33)—(35) and 21 C.F.R. §§ 1300.02(b)(17)—(19) (defining listed chemicals).

[25] 21 C.F.R. § 1300.02(b)(18) defines the term "List I chemical" as "a chemical specifically designated by the Administrator in [21 C.F.R.] § 1310.02(a) ... that, in addition to legitimate uses, is used in manufacturing a controlled substance in violation of the [CSA] and is important to the manufacture of a controlled substance."

[26] 21 C.F.R. § 1300.02(b)(19) defines the term "List II chemical" as "a chemical, other than a List I chemical, specifically designated by the Administrator in [21 C.F.R.] § 1310.02(b) ... that, in addition to legitimate uses, is used in manufacturing a controlled substance in violation of the [CSA]."

[27] 21 C.F.R. § 1300.02(b)(18).

[28] 21 U.S.C. §§ 802(32)(A) and (B).

[29] *See* 21 U.S.C. § 813 ("A controlled substance analogue shall, to the extent intended for human consumption, be treated, for the purposes of any Federal law as a controlled substance in schedule I").

[30] United Nations Office on Drugs and Crime, *Synthetic Drugs*, *at* http://www.apaic.org/index.php?option=com_content&view=article&id=91&Itemid=63.

[31] *Drug Enforcement Administration, Schedules of Controlled Substances: Temporary Placement of Three Synthetic Cathinones Into Schedule I*, 76 Fed. Reg. 65371 (Oct. 21, 2011).

[32] For more information on this law and this topic generally, *see* CRS Report R42066, *Synthetic Drugs: Overview and Issues for Congress*, by Kristin M. Finklea and Lisa N. Sacco.

[33] The procedures for these scheduling actions are found at 21 U.S.C. § 811(d).

[34] Drug Enforcement Administration, *Electronic Prescriptions for Controlled Substances,* 75 Fed. Reg. 16235, 16237 (Mar. 31, 2010).

[35] According to 21 C.F.R. § 1300.02(b)(24), the term "registrant" means "any person who is registered [with the DEA] pursuant to [21 U.S.C. §§ 823 or 957]."

[36] DEA, *Disposal of Controlled Substances by Persons Not Registered With the Drug Enforcement Administration,* 74 Fed. Reg. 3480, 3481 (January 21, 2009).

[37] DEA, *Definition and Registration of Reverse Distributors*, 70 Fed. Reg. 22591 (May 2, 2005).

[38] 21 U.S.C. § 822; 21 C.F.R. Part 1301.

[39] 21 C.F.R. §§ 1301.22-1301.24 (exempting agents of registrants, certain military personnel, and law enforcement officials from DEA registration requirements).

[40] 21 U.S.C. § 802(27).

[41] 21 U.S.C. § 822(c)(3).

[42] DEA, *Definition and Registration of Reverse Distributors*, 68 Fed. Reg. 41222, 41226 (proposed July 11, 2003).

[43] 21 C.F.R. § 822(a).

[44] 21 C.F.R. § 1301.13.

[45] *Id.*

[46] 21 U.S.C. § 821; *see also* 21 C.F.R. § 1301.13(e)(1) (chart detailing specific types of registrations and respective fees).

[47] 21 U.S.C. § 822(f); 21 C.F.R. § 1301.31.

[48] 21 U.S.C. § 823.

[49] 21 U.S.C. §§ 823(a)-(f).

[50] 21 U.S.C. § 824(a) states in pertinent part: "A registration pursuant to section 823 of this title to manufacture, distribute, or dispense a controlled substance or a list I chemical may be suspended or revoked by the [Administrator] upon a finding that the registrant—

(1) has materially falsified any application filed pursuant to or required by this subchapter or subchapter II of this chapter;

(2) has been convicted of a felony under this subchapter or subchapter II of this chapter or any other law of the United States, or of any State, relating to any substance defined in this subchapter as a controlled substance or a list I chemical;

(3) has had his State license or registration suspended, revoked, or denied by competent State authority and is no longer authorized by State law to engage in the manufacturing, distribution, or dispensing of controlled substances or list I chemicals or has had the suspension, revocation, or denial recommended by competent State authority;

(4) has committed such acts as would render his registration under section 823 of this title inconsistent with the public interest as determined under such section; or

(5) has been excluded (or directed to be excluded) from participation in a program pursuant to section 1320a—7(a) of [the Social Security Act, which excludes certain individuals and entities from participation in Medicare and State healthcare programs] . . ."

[51] 21 U.S.C. § 824(c).

[52] 21 U.S.C. § 824(d); 21 C.F.R. § 1301.36(e).

[53] THOMAS C. FOX, CAROL COLBORN LOEPERE & JOSEPH W. METRO, HEALTH CARE FINANCIAL TRANSACTIONS MANUAL § 20:62 (2005).

[54] 21 C.F.R. § 1301.52.

[55] 21 C.F.R. § 1301.52(b).

[56] 21 C.F.R. § 1301.12.

[57] *See* United States v. Clinical Leasing Service, Inc., 925 F.2d 120 (5th Cir. 1991).

[58] Section 3(b) of P.L. 110-425, amending 21 U.S.C. § 823(f).

[59] 21 U.S.C. § 827; 21 C.F.R. Part 1304.

[60] 21 U.S.C. § 827(a)(3); 21 C.F.R. § 1304.21(a).

[61] 21 U.S.C. § 827(b)(3); 21 C.F.R. § 1304.04(a).

[62] *Id.*

[63] 21 U.S.C. § 842(a)(5).

[64] 21 U.S.C. § 843(a)(4).
[65] *See generally* 21 C.F.R. Part 1310 (records and reports of listed chemicals).
[66] 21 U.S.C. § 830(a) and (b); 21 C.F.R. §§ 1310.03-06.
[67] *See* chart at 21 C.F.R. § 1310.12(c).
[68] For the purposes of the CSA, the term "distribute," as defined by 21 U.S.C. § 802(11), means "to deliver (other than by administering or dispensing [to an ultimate user or research subject]) a controlled substance or listed chemical."
[69] 21 C.F.R. Part 1305.
[70] DEA Form 222 is only issued to customers who are properly registered with the DEA.
[71] 21 C.F.R. § 1305.13(c).
[72] 21 C.F.R. § 1305.13(d).
[73] 21 C.F.R. § 1305 Subpart C.
[74] 21 C.F.R. § 1305.29.
[75] 21 C.F.R. §§ 1304.31 and 1304.32.
[76] 21 C.F.R. § 1304.33.
[77] 21 C.F.R. § 1304.33(d).
[78] Section 3(c) of the Ryan Haight Online Pharmacy Consumer Protection Act of 2008, P.L. 110-425, adding new 21 U.S.C. § 827(d)(2). However, pharmacies are exempt from such reporting requirement if they do not exceed in a given month either of two thresholds: (1) 100 or more prescriptions dispensed, or (2) 5,000 or more dosage units of all controlled substances combined. *Id.*
[79] An "online pharmacy" means a person, entity, or Internet site, whether in the United States or abroad, that knowingly or intentionally delivers, distributes, or dispenses, or offers or attempts to deliver, distribute, or dispense, a controlled substance by means of the Internet, but does *not* include, among other things, (1) manufacturers and distributors who do not dispense controlled substances to an unregistered individual or entity, (2) advertisements that do not attempt to facilitate an actual transaction involving a controlled substance, or (3) a registered pharmacy whose dispensing of controlled substances via the Internet consists solely of refilling or filling new prescriptions for controlled substances in schedule III, IV, or V. 21 U.S.C. § 802(52), as added by section 3(a) of P.L. 110-425.
[80] Section 3(d) of P.L. 110-425, adding new § 311 to the Controlled Substances Act.
[81] *Id.*
[82] According to 21 U.S.C. § 802(10), the term "dispense" means "to deliver a controlled substance to an ultimate user or research subject by, or pursuant to the lawful order of, a practitioner, including the prescribing and administering of a controlled substance and the packaging, labeling or compounding necessary to prepare the substance for such delivery."
[83] According to 21 U.S.C. § 802(21), the term "practitioner" means "a physician, dentist, veterinarian, scientific investigator, pharmacy, hospital, or other person licensed, registered, or otherwise permitted, by the United States or the jurisdiction in which he practices or does research, to distribute, dispense, conduct research with respect to, administer, or use in teaching or chemical analysis, a controlled substance in the course of professional practice or research."
[84] *See* 21 C.F.R. § 1306.03 (persons entitled to issue prescriptions).
[85] 21 C.F.R. § 1306.04; United States v. Moore, 4223 U.S. 122 (1975).
[86] Pharmacists share with practitioners the responsibility to ensure that controlled substances are properly prescribed and dispensed. Both practitioners and pharmacists are subject to the criminal and civil provisions of the CSA for knowingly prescribing and dispensing a controlled substance in a manner inconsistent with the act. 21 C.F.R. § 1306.04(a).
[87] 21 U.S.C. § 829(a); *see also* 21 C.F.R. § 1306.05 (manner of issuance of prescriptions for Schedule II controlled substances).
[88] 21 U.S.C. § 829(a); *see also* 21 C.F.R. § 1306.11(b) (authorizing individual practitioners to administer or dispense controlled substances directly to patients without prescription).
[89] 21 C.F.R. § 290.10.

[90] 21 C.F.R. § 1306.11(d).

[91] 21 C.F.R. § 1306.05.

[92] 21 U.S.C. § 829(b). If the prescription is made orally, the pharmacist must promptly reduce to writing all of the information required to be in a prescription under 21 C.F.R. § 1306.05, except for the signature of the practitioner. 21 C.F.R. § 1306.21(a).

[93] 21 U.S.C. § 829(b); 21 C.F.R. § 1306.21(b).

[94] Drug Enforcement Administration, *Electronic Prescriptions for Controlled Substances,* 75 Fed. Reg. 16235, 16307 (Mar. 31, 2010).

[95] *See* 21 C.F.R. § 1306.13(a) ("The partial filling of a prescription for a substance listed in Schedule II is permissible if the pharmacist is unable to supply the full quantity called for in a written or emergency oral prescription.... The remaining portion of the prescription may be filled within 72 hours of the first partial filling").

[96] 21 U.S.C. § 829(a)("No prescription for a controlled substance in schedule II may be refilled.").

[97] 21 U.S.C. 829(b); 21 C.F.R. § 1306.22(a).

[98] Drug Enforcement Administration, *Electronic Prescriptions for Controlled Substances,* 75 Fed. Reg. 16235, 16316 (Mar. 31, 2010).

[99] Section 2 of the Ryan Haight Online Pharmacy Consumer Protection Act of 2008, P.L. 110-425, adding new 21 U.S.C. § 829(e).

[100] *Id.*

[101] *See* 21 U.S.C. §§ 826(a)-(e) (general provisions regarding the establishment of production quotas for Schedule I and II controlled substances).

[102] 21 C.F.R. §§ 1303.11(b)(1)-(5).

[103] *See* 21 C.F.R. § 1301.71 (general security requirements and standards for measuring compliance).

[104] 21 C.F.R. § 1301.71(b) states: "Substantial compliance with the standards set forth in §§ 1301.72-1301.76 may be deemed sufficient by the Administrator after evaluation of the overall security system and needs of the applicant or registrant." Section 1301.71(b) also sets forth a list of fifteen discretionary factors for Administrator to consider when evaluating the overall security system of an applicant or registrant; *see also* 21 C.F.R. § 1309.71(a)-(c) (general security requirements for List I chemicals).

[105] 21 C.F.R. § 1301.71(c).

[106] *See* 21 C.F.R. §§ 1301.72(a)(1)(i)-(iii) (specifications required for safes and steel cabinets storing Schedule I and II drugs or substances); *see also* 21 C.F.R. §§ 1301.72(a)(2) and 1301.72(a)(3)(i)-(vi) (specifications required for vaults storing Schedule I and II drugs or substances).

[107] *See* 21 C.F.R. § 1301.75 (physical security controls for practitioners).

[108] 21 C.F.R. § 1301.76(b).

[109] 21 C.F.R. § 1301.76(a).

[110] 21 C.F.R. § 1301.90.

[111] For information about disposal by patients who possess already dispensed controlled substances (as opposed to DEA registrants that want to dispose of them), *see* CRS Report R40548, *Legal Issues Relating to the Disposal of Dispensed Controlled Substances*, by Brian T. Yeh. This report discusses the Secure and Responsible Drug Disposal Act of 2010, P.L. 111-273, which, among other things, amended the Controlled Substances Act to allow a patient to deliver controlled substances to an entity that is authorized by federal law to dispose of them, providing that such disposal occurs in accordance with regulations issued by the Attorney General to prevent diversion of controlled substances.

[112] DEA, *Definition and Registration of Reverse Distributors*, 70 Fed. Reg. 22591, 22592 (May 2, 2005).

[113] Under 21 C.F.R. § 1307.21, any person may request permission from DEA to dispose of controlled substances without the need for a DEA or state government witness. If a registrant has a regular need to dispose of controlled substances, the DEA may grant blanket

authorization for such disposal; however, "DEA normally requires that the registrant provide two designated responsible individuals to accompany the drugs to the disposal site and witness the destruction." DEA, *Definition and Registration of Reverse Distributors*, 70 Fed. Reg. 22591 (May 2, 2005).

[114] A "reverse distributor" is a DEA-registered entity "who receives controlled substances acquired from another DEA registrant for the purpose of—(1) returning unwanted, unusable, or outdated controlled substances to the manufacturer or the manufacturer's agent; or (2) where necessary, processing such substances or arranging for processing such substances for disposal." 21 C.F.R. § 1300.01(b)(41).

[115] For a description of the criminal penalty provisions of the CSA, *see* CRS Report RL30722, *Drug Offenses: Maximum Fines and Terms of Imprisonment for Violation of the Federal Controlled Substances Act and Related Laws*, by Brian T. Yeh.

[116] 21 U.S.C. §§ 841(c); (e)-(f).

[117] 21 U.S.C. § 842.

[118] 21 U.S.C. § 843.

[119] 21 U.S.C. § 842(a)(2).

[120] 21 U.S.C. § 842(a)(5).

[121] 21 U.S.C. § 842(a)(6).

[122] *See generally* 21 U.S.C. § 842(c) (penalties for committing prohibited acts set forth in § 842(a)).

[123] 21 U.S.C. § 843(a)(1).

[124] 21 U.S.C. § 843(a)(2).

[125] 21 U.S.C. § 843(a)(4)(A).

[126] 21 U.S.C. § 843(a)(4)(B).

[127] *See generally* 21 U.S.C. § 843(d) (penalties for committing prohibited acts set forth in § 843(a)).

[128] 21 U.S.C. § 843(f).

[129] 21 U.S.C. §§ 841(c)(1)-(3).

[130] *See* 21 U.S.C. § 841(f)(1) and (2) (penalties for offenses involving listed chemicals).

[131] 21 U.S.C. § 841(e).

[132] 21 C.F.R. § 1301.24(a)(1).

[133] 21 C.F.R. § 1301.24(a)(2). For additional registration exceptions, see 21 C.F.R. §§ 1301.22-1301.23.

[134] 21 U.S.C. § 822(c).

[135] 21 C.F.R. § 1301.11(a); 21 U.S.C. § 822(c).

[136] 21 U.S.C. § 822(d).

[137] 21 U.S.C. §§ 827(c)(1)(A), 827(c)(1)(B).

[138] 21 U.S.C. § 827(c)(2).

In: Recreational and Medical Marijuana ISBN: 978-1-62808-114-5
Editors: Valentin Dijkstra

Chapter 4

DRUG OFFENSES: MAXIMUM FINES AND TERMS OF IMPRISONMENT FOR VIOLATION OF THE FEDERAL CONTROLLED SUBSTANCES ACT AND RELATED LAWS*

Brian T. Yeh

SUMMARY

This is a chart of the maximum fines and terms of imprisonment that may be imposed as a consequence of conviction for violation of the federal Controlled Substances Act (CSA) and other drug supply and drug demand related laws.

It lists the penalties for: heroin, cocaine, crack, PCP, LSD, marihuana (marijuana), amphetamine, methamphetamine, listed (precursor) chemicals, paraphernalia, date rape drugs, rave drugs, designer drugs, ecstasy, drug kingpins, as well as the other substances including narcotics and opiates assigned to Schedule I, Schedule II, Schedule III, Schedule IV, and Schedule V of the Controlled Substances Act and the Controlled

---

* This is an edited, reformatted and augmented version of a Congressional Research Service publication, CRS Report for Congress RL30722, prepared for Members and Committees of Congress, from www.crs.gov, dated December 13, 2012.

Substances Import and Export Act (Title II and Title III of the Comprehensive Drug Abuse and Control Act).

It maps the penalty structure for violations of 21 U.S.C. 841 (drug trafficking), 21 U.S.C. 841(b)(5) (cultivation on federal property), 21 U.S.C. 841(b)(6) (environmental damage from illegal manufacturing), 21 U.S.C. 841(b)(7) (crime of violence), 21 U.S.C. 841(c) (offenses involving listed chemicals), 21 U.S.C. 841(d) (booby traps on federal lands), 21 U.S.C. 841(f) (distribution/possession of listed chemicals), 21 U.S.C. 841(g) (Internet sales of date rape drugs), 21 U.S.C. 841(h) (dispensing controlled substances that are prescription drugs by means of the Internet), 21 U.S.C. 842 (regulatory offenses), 21 U.S.C. 843 (communications-related offenses), 21 U.S.C. 844 (simple possession), 21 U.S.C. 846, 963 (attempt and conspiracy), 21 U.S.C. 849 (drug dealing at truck stops), 21 U.S.C. 848 (continuing criminal enterprises (CCE)), 21 U.S.C. 854, 855 (investment of illicit drug profits), 21 U.S.C. 856 (establishing manufacturing operations), 21 U.S.C. 858 (endangering human life), 21 U.S.C. 859 (distribution to infants, minors, children, juveniles, and those under 18 years of age), 21 U.S.C. 860 (distribution in school zones), 21 U.S.C. 861 (distribution to pregnant women), 21 U.S.C. 863 (trafficking in drug paraphernalia), 21 U.S.C. 864 (theft of anhydrous ammonia, or transportation of stolen anhydrous ammonia), 21 U.S.C. 865 (smuggling methamphetamine into the United States), 21 U.S.C. 960 (illicit drug import and export), 21 U.S.C. 960a (narco-terrorism), 21 U.S.C. 962 (recalcitrant drug smugglers), 21 U.S.C. 1906 (financial transactions with designated foreign narcotics traffickers), 18 U.S.C. 545 (smuggling goods into the United States), 18 U.S.C. 546 (smuggling goods into foreign countries), 18 U.S.C. 924(c) (firearms and armor piercing ammunition in connection to drug trafficking crime), 18 U.S.C. 924(e) (armed career criminals), 18 U.S.C. 1952 (Travel Act), 18 U.S.C. 1956 (money laundering), 18 U.S.C. 1957 (monetary transactions in property derived from unlawful activity), 18 U.S.C. 1959 (compensated crime of violence in aid of racketeering), 18 U.S.C. 1963 (racketeering (RICO)), 18 U.S.C. 2118 (robberies and burglaries involving controlled substances), 18 U.S.C. 3559(c) (three strikes), 19 U.S.C. 1590 (aviation smuggling), 26 U.S.C. 7201 (tax evasion), 26 U.S.C. 7203 (failure to file required returns), 26 U.S.C. 7206 (fraud and false statements), 31 U.S.C. 5322 (currency transaction reporting (smurfing)), 31 U.S.C. 5332 (bulk cash smuggling into or out of the United States), 46 U.S.C. 70506 (maritime drug law enforcement).

This report reflects amendments to the Controlled Substances Act made by the Fair Sentencing Act of 2010 (P.L. 111-220) that increased the quantities of crack cocaine necessary to trigger certain penalties and also increased the fine amounts for major drug traffickers.

Trafficking

Unlawful distribution, possession with intent to distribute, manufacture, importation and exportation, etc. (21 U.S.C. 841, 960, 962, and 46 U.S.C. 70506)[1]		
1st offense		
Substance Amount	Fine	Imprisonment
Heroin		
1 kilogram[2] or more	$10/50 million	10 years to life
100 to 999 grams	$5/25 million	5 to 40 years
Less than 100 grams	$1/5 million	Up to 20 years
Coca leaf and derivatives		
5 kilograms or more	$10/50 million	10 years to life
500 to 4999 grams	$5/25 million	5 to 40 years
Less than 500 grams	$1/5 million	Up to 20 years
Ecgonine (a cocaine precursor)		
5 kilograms or more	$10/50 million	10 years to life
500 to 4999 grams	$5/25 million	5 to 40 years
Less than 500 grams	$1/5 million	Up to 20 years
Coca leaves, cocaine, or ecgonine containing cocaine base		
("Crack," etc.)		
280 grams or more	$10/50 million	10 years to life
28 to 279 grams	$5/25 million	5 to 40 years
Less than 28 grams	$1/5 million	Up to 20 years
PCP (phencyclidine)		
100 grams or more	$10/50 million	10 years to life
10 to 99 grams	$5/25 million	5 to 40 years
Less than 10 grams	$1/5 million	Up to 20 years
Mixture or substance containing detectable amount of PCP		
1 kilogram or more	$10/50 million	10 years to life

100 to 999 grams	$5/25 million	5 to 40 years
Less than 100 grams	$1/5 million	Up to 20 years
LSD (lysergic acid diethylamide)		
10 grams or more	$10/50 million	10 years to life
1 to 9 grams	$5/25 million	5 to 40 years
Less than 1 gram	$1/5 million	Up to 20 years
N-phenyl-N-[1-(2-phenylethyl)-4-piperidinyl] propanamide (Fentanyl, i.e., "synthetic heroin") 400 grams or more (or 100 grams or more of a mixture or substance containing a detectable amount of any analogue of it)	$10/50 million	10 years to life
40 to 399 grams (or 10-99 grams of a mixture containing a detectable amount of any analogue of it)	$5/25 million	5 to 40 years
Less than 40 grams	$1/5 million	Up to 20 years
Marihuana		
1000 kilograms or more or 1000 or more plants[3]	$10/50 million	10 years to life
100 to 999 kilograms or 100 to 999 plants	$5/25 million	5 to 40 years
50 to 99 kilograms or 50 to 99 plants	$1/5 million	Up to 20 years
Under 50 kilograms4, 10 kilograms of hashish, 1 kilogram of hashish oil, or 1 to 49 plants	$250,000/$1 million	Up to 5 years
Methamphetamine		
50 grams or more or 500 grams or more of a mixture	$10/50 million	10 years to life
5 to 49 grams or 50 to 499 grams of a mixture	$5/25 million	5 to 40 years
Less than 5 grams or less than 50 grams of a mixture	$1/5 million	Up to 20 years
Gamma hydroxybutyric acid		
any weight	$1/5 million	Up to 20 years
Flunitrazepam[5]		
1 gram	$1/5 million	Up to 20 years
Less than 1 gram	$250,000/$1 million	Up to 5 years
Any other Schedule I or II substance		
any weight	$1/5 million	Up to 20 years
Any other Schedule III substance		

any weight	$500,000/$2.5 million	Up to 15 years6
Any other Schedule IV substance		
any weight	$250,000/$1 million	Up to 5 years7
Any Schedule V substance		
any weight	$100,000/$250,000	Up to 1 year
2nd offense[8]		
Heroin		
1 kilogram or more	$20/75 million	20 years to life
100 to 999 grams	$8/50 million	10 years to life
Less than 100 grams	$2/10 million	Up to 30 years
Coca leaf and derivatives		
5 kilograms or more	$20/75 million	20 years to life
500 to 4999 grams	$8/50 million	10 years to life
Less than 500 grams	$2/10 million	Up to 30 years
Ecgonine (a cocaine precursor)		
5 kilograms or more	$20/75 million	20 years to life
500 to 4999 grams	$8/50 million	10 years to life
Less than 500 grams	$2/10 million	Up to 30 years
Coca leaves, cocaine, or ecgonine containing cocaine base ("Crack," etc.)		
280 grams or more	$20/75 million	20 years to life
28 to 279 grams	$8/50 million	10 years to life
Less than 28 grams	$2/10 million	Up to 30 years
PCP (phencyclidine)		
100 grams or more	$20/75 million	20 years to life
10 to 99 grams	$8/50 million	10 years to life
Less than 10 grams	$2/10 million	Up to 30 years
Mixture or substance containing detectable amount of PCP 1 kilogram or more $20/75 million 20 years to life		
100 to 999 grams	$8/50 million	10 years to life
Less than 100 grams	$2/10 million	Up to 30 years
LSD(lysergic acid diethylamide) 10 grams or more	$20/75 million	20 years to life
1 to 9 grams	$8/50 million	10 years to life
Less than 1 gram	$2/10 million	Up to 30 years
N-phenyl-N-[1-(2-phenylethyl)-4-		

piperidinyl] propanamide		
(Fentanyl, i.e., "synthetic heroin") 400 grams or more (or		
100 grams or more of a mixture or substance containing a		
detectable amount of any analogue of it)	$20/75 million	20 years to life
40 to 399 grams (or 10-99 grams of a mixture		
containing a detectable amount of any analogue		
of it)	$8/50 million	10 years to life
Less than 40 grams	$2/10 million	Up to 30 years
Marihuana		
1000 kilograms or more or 1000 or more		
plants)	$20/75 million	20 years to life
100 to 999 kilograms or 100 to 999 plants)	$8/50 million	10 years to life
50 to 99 kilograms or 50 to 99 plants9	$2/10 million	Up to 30 years
Less than 50 kilograms,10 10 kilograms of		
hashish, 1 kilogram of hashish oil, or 1 to 49		
plants	$500,000/$2 million	Up to 10 years
Methamphetamine 50 grams or more	$20/75 million	20 years to life
5 to 49 grams	$8/50 million	10 years to life
Less than 5 grams	$2/10 million	Up to 30 years
Gamma hydroxybutyric acid any weight	$2/10 million	Up to 30 years
Flunitrazepam11 1 gram	$2/10 million	Up to 30 years
Less than 1 gram	$500,000/$2 million	Up to 10 years
Any other Schedule I or II substance any weight	$2/10 million	Up to 30 years
Any other Schedule III substance any weight	$1 million/$5 million	Up to 30 years
Any other Schedule IV substance		
any weight	$500,000/$2 million	Up to 10 years
Any Schedule V substance		
any weight	$200,000/$500,000	Up to 4 years

3rd offense		
A Schedule I or II substance singled out for special penalty treatment (as indicated above) in amounts constituting a top level offense	Same as 2nd offense	Life
Cultivation on Federal property (21 U.S.C. 841(b)(5))		
Any offense		
All substances/all weights	Greater of $500,000/ $1 million or the maximum	Maximum term for distribution of the
	fine for distribution of the	substance involved
	substance involved	
Environmental damage on Federal property resulting from controlled substance manufacturing or distribution (21 U.S.C. 841(b)(6))		
Any offense[12]		
All substances	Up to $250,000	Up to 5 years
Offenses involving essential (listed) chemicals, generally (21 U.S.C. 841(c))		
Any offense[13]		
List I chemicals [under 21 U.S.C. 802(34)]	Up to $250,000	Up to 20 years
List II chemicals [under 21 U.S.C. 802(35)]	Up to $250,000	Up to 10 years
Wrongful distribution or possession of essential (listed) chemicals (21 U.S.C. 841(f))		
Knowing unlawful distribution		
Listed chemicals [under 21 U.S.C. 802 (33)]	Up to $250,000	Up to 5 years
Knowing possession of unreported listed chemicals		
Listed chemicals [under 21 U.S.C. 802 (33)]	Up to $100,000	Up to 1 year
Internet Sales of Date Rape Drugs (21 U.S.C. 841(g))		

Knowingly using the Internet to distribute a date rape drug[14]	Up to $250,000	Up to 20 years
Dispensing Controlled Substances by Means of the		
Internet (21 U.S.C. 841(h))		
Knowingly or intentionally using the Internet to deliver, distribute, or dispense a controlled substance without a valid prescription[15] (or aiding or abetting such activity)	Sentences determined according to the penalties authorized under 21 U.S.C. 841(b)[16]	
Regulatory offenses & use of communications to facilitate distribution (21 U.S.C. 842, 843)		
1st offense Generally[17]	Up to $100,000	Up to 1 year
Deception offenses, etc.[18]	Up to $250,000	Up to 4 years
Methamphetamine equipment offenses	Up to $250,000	Up to 10 years
Advertisement offenses[19]	Up to $250,000	Up to 4 years
2nd offense Generally	Up to $250,000	Up to 2 years
Deception offenses, etc.	Up to $250,000	Up to 8 years
Methamphetamine equipment offenses	Up to $60,000	Up to 20 years
Advertisement offenses	Up to $250,000	Up to 8 years
Manufacturing or Distributing Controlled Substances		
Within 1000 Feet of a Truck Stop or Highway Rest Area (21 U.S.C. 849)		
1st offense All substances	Up to twice the penalties otherwise authorized	
2nd offense All substances	Up to three times the penalties otherwise authorized	
Distribution to persons under age 21 by those age 18		
or older (21 U.S.C. 859)		
1st offense All substances	Up to twice the penalties otherwise authorized[20]	
2nd offense All substances	Up to three times the penalties otherwise authorized	
Distribution or manufacturing in or near schools, colleges, or certain youth-centered recreational facilities (21 U.S.C. 860, 860a)[21]		

1st offense All substances (except methamphetamine)	Up to twice the penalties otherwise authorized for distribution or manufacture but at least 1 year in prison[22]	
2nd offense All substances (except methamphetamine)	Up to three times the penalties otherwise authorized for distribution or manufacture but at least 3 years in prison	
Any offense involving methamphetamine	Other sentence as imposed plus imprisonment for no more than 20 years	
Trafficking in drug paraphernalia (21 U.S.C. 863)		
Interstate or foreign sale and transportation of, or use of the		
mails to sell, drug paraphernalia	Up to $250,000	Up to 3 years

Possession

Simple possession (21 U.S.C. 844)23		
1st offense	Not less than $1,000	Up to 1 year
2nd offense24	Not less than $2,500	15 days to 2 years
3rd offense	Not less than $5,000	90 days to 3 years
Any offense		
Flunitrazepam	Up to $250,000	Up to 3 years

Controlled Substance Violations and Other Crimes/Activity

Attempt and conspiracy (21 U.S.C. 846, 963)		
Any offense All substances	Same as penalties for the underlying	
	offense	

Use of a controlled substance to commit a crime of violence (21		
U.S.C. 841(b)(7))		
Any offense25 All substances	Up to $250,000	Up to 20 years
Boobytraps on Federal property (21 U.S.C. 841(d))[26]		
1st offense	Up to $250,000	Up to 10 years
2nd offense	Up to $250,000	Up to 20 years
Continuing Criminal Enterprise (CCE) ("kingpin")		
(21 U.S.C. 848)[27]		
1st offense All substances	Up to $2 million	20 years to life
2nd offense All substances	Up to $4 million	30 years to life
Any offense, if the offender is a major participant, involving an enterprise		
that grosses $10 million a year or more or involving 300 times28 the amount of controlled substances required to trigger the most severe distribution penalties of 21 U.S.C. 841 All substances		
	Up to $4 million	life
Establishing manufacturing operations (21 U.S.C. 856)		
Opening, maintaining, financing or making available a place for unlawful		
manufacture, distribution or use of controlled substances All substances	Up to $500,000	Up to 20 years
Endangering human life while illegally manufacturing a		
controlled substance (21 U.S.C. 858)		
Any offense All substances	Up to $250,000	Up to 10 years
Employment of persons under 18 years of age (for violation of the CSA) or unauthorized distribution to a pregnant individual		
(21 U.S.C. 861)		
1st offense Generally Up to twice the penalties otherwise authorized for		
the underlying offense but at least 1 year in prison[29]		

2nd offense Generally Up to three times the penalties otherwise authorized for the underlying offense but at least 1 year in prison[30]		
Any offense Use of person under 14 or distribution to a person under 18	Up to $50,000 Up to 5 years	
Narco-Terrorism (21 U.S.C. 960a)		
Engaging in prohibited drug activity knowing or intending to provide	Up to $250,000	At least twice the
anything of pecuniary value to terrorists		minimum
		punishment
		authorized under 21
		U.S.C. 841(b)(1)
Theft of anhydrous ammonia, or transportation of stolen		
anhydrous ammonia with intent or knowledge that such will be		
used to manufacture a controlled substance (21 U.S.C. 864)		
1st offense	Up to $250,000	Up to 4 years
2nd offense	Up to $250,000	Up to 8 years
Violation of regulations proscribing financial transactions with		
significant foreign narcotics traffickers (21 U.S.C. 1906)		
Any offense (individual)	Up to $250,000	Up to 10 years
Any offense (organization)	Up to $10,000,000	
Any offense (organization officer or agent)	Up to $5,000,000	Up to 30 years
Travel Act: use of interstate facilities in aid of a racketeering enterprise involving controlled substances (18 U.S.C. 1952)		
Any substance and the intent to commit the following act:		
A crime of violence in furtherance of the racketeering enterprise	Up to $250,000	Up to 20 years, or any term of years or life if death

		results
Distributing the proceeds from the racketeering enterprise	Up to $250,000	Up to 5 years
Promotion or facilitation of the racketeering enterprise Up to $250,000		Up to 5 years
Use or possession of firearms or armor piercing ammunition in connection to a drug trafficking crime (18 U.S.C. 924(c))31		
1st offense involving a firearm		
Generally		Not less than 5 years
If a firearm is brandished		Not less than 7 years
If a firearm is discharged		Not less than 10 years
If firearm is a short-barreled rifle, short-barreled shotgun, or semiautomatic assault weapon		Not less than 10 years
If firearm is a machinegun or destructive device, or equipped with a silencer/muffler		Not less than 30 years
2nd or subsequent offense involving a firearm		
Generally		Not less than 25 years life
If firearm is a machinegun or destructive device, or equipped with a silencer/muffler		
Any offense involving armor piercing ammunition		
Use or possession		Not less than 15 years
If such ammunition is used for murder		Any term of years or life
If such ammunition is used for manslaughter	Up to $250,000	Up to 10 years
If such ammunition is used for manslaughter	Up to $250,000	Up to 6 years
Robberies Involving Controlled Substances (18 U.S.C. 2118(a))		
Any offense		
Any quantity of a controlled substance in the care, custody, control, or possession of a DEA registrant, if (1) the replacement cost	Up to $250,000	Up to 20 years

of such material is not less than $500, (2) the robber (or person who attempted		
to rob the substance) traveled in interstate or foreign commerce or used any facility in interstate/foreign commerce to facilitate such unlawful taking, or (3) another person was killed or suffered significant bodily injury due to the robbery or attempted robbery		
If the person committing this offense assaults any person (or jeopardizes the life of any person) by using a dangerous weapon	Up to $250,000	Up to 25 years
If the person committing this offense kills any person	Up to $250,000	Any term of years or life
Burglaries Involving Controlled Substances (18 U.S.C. 2118(b))		
Any offense		
Any quantity of a controlled substance in the business premises or property of a DEA registrant, if (1) the replacement cost of such material is not less than $500, (2) the burglar (or person who attempted to burglarize the premises) traveled in interstate or foreign commerce or used any facility in commerce or used any facility in interstate/foreign commerce to facilitate such unlawful entry, or (3) another person was killed or suffered significant bodily injury due to the burglary or attempted burglary	Up to $250,000	Up to 20 years
If the person committing this offense assaults any person (or jeopardizes the life of any person) by using a dangerous weapon	Up to $250,000	Up to 25 years
If the person committing this offense kills any person	Up to $250,000	Any term of years or life
Conspiracy to Commit Robbery or Burglary Involving Controlled Substances (18 U.S.C. 2118(d))		
Any offense		
If two or more persons conspire to violate 18 U.S.C. 2118(a) or 2118(b), and one or more	Up to $250,000	Up to 10 years

of such persons performs any overt act to effect the object of the conspiracy		
Armed career criminal: possession of a firearm by a convicted felon or other disqualified person with 3 or more prior serious controlled substance convictions (drug crimes punishable by imprisonment for 10 years or more) or prior violent crime convictions (18 U.S.C. 924(e))		
Any offense		
All substances	Up to $250,000	Not less than 15 years
Three strikes: commission of a serious violent felony by an individual with a prior serious controlled substance conviction (drug kingpin or most seriously punished trafficking offense) and a prior serious violent felony conviction or 2 or more prior serious violent felony convictions (18 U.S.C. 3559(c))		
Any offense		
All substances	Up to $250,000	life

Racketeering

Commission of a pattern of racketeering activity including one or more narcotic or dangerous drug felony to invest in, acquire, operate or participate in the affairs of an interstate enterprise ((RICO)(18 U.S.C. 1963))		
Any offense Narcotic and dangerous drugs	Up to $250,000	Up to 20 years or life
		if the maximum for
		the predicate is life
Compensated crime of violence in aid of RICO (18 U.S.C. 1959)		

Any offense involving any substance and the following criminal act: Murder	Up to $250,000	life
Kidnapping	Up to $250,000	Up to life in prison
Maiming	Up to $250,000	Up to 30 years
Serious injury	Up to $250,000	Up to 20 years
Threats	Up to $250,000	Up to 5 years
Attempt or conspiracy to murder or kidnap	Up to $250,000	Up to 10 years
Attempt or conspiracy to maim or commit a serious assault	Up to $250,000	Up to 3 years

Smuggling

Smuggling Goods into the United States (18 U.S.C. 545)		
Any offense		
All substances	Up to $250,000	Up to 20 years
Smuggling Goods into Foreign Countries (18 U.S.C. 546)		
Any offense		
All substances	Up to $250,000	Up to 2 years
Smuggling methamphetamine or methamphetamine precursor chemicals into the United States while using facilitated entry programs (21 U.S.C. 865)		
Any offense	Imprisonment Sentence for Methamphetamine Offense Enhanced By Up to 15 years	
Smuggling a controlled substance by using an aircraft to transport it (19 U.S.C. 1590)[32]		
Any offense		
All substances	Up to $250,000	Up to 20 years

Laundering Money from Controlled Substance Violations

Laundering (18 U.S.C. 1956)		
Any offense		

All substances	Up to greater of $500,000 or 2X the amount of $ laundered	Up to 20 years
Monetary traffic in property derived from unlawful activity (18 U.S.C. 1957)		
Any offense		
All substances	Up to greater of $250,000 or 2X the amount of $ laundered	Up to 10 years
Currency transaction and transportation reporting (31 U.S.C. 5322)		
1st offense		
All substances	Up to $250,000	Up to 5 years
2nd offense		
All substances	Up to $500,000	Up to 10 years
Bulk cash smuggling into or out of the United States (31 U.S.C. 5332)		
Knowingly concealing more than $ 10,000 across a U.S. border		Up to 5 years
Investment of illicit drug profits (21 U.S.C. 854, 855)		
Any offense		
All substances	Up to the greater of 2X profit/proceeds or $50,000	Up to 10 years

Tax Offenses

Attempted evasion [concerning income from controlled substance violations] (26 U.S.C. 7201)		
Any offense		
All substances	Up to $250,000	Up to 5 years
Willful failure to file return [concerning income for such violations] (26 U.S.C. 7203)		

Any offense		
All substances	Up to $250,000	Up to 5 years
Fraud and false statements [concerning income from such violations] (26 U.S.C. 7206)		
Any offense		
All substances	Up to $250,000	Up to 3 years

End Notes

[1] All trafficking offenses involving Schedule I and II substances (and gamma hydrobutyric acid and flunitrazepam) are subject to the same imprisonment penalty—20 years to life—if death or serious bodily injury results from the use of the substance involved. Unless otherwise indicated, weights apply to any mixture containing a detectable amount of the substance regardless of the weight of the substance in the mixture. A reference to a fine of "$5/25 million" means a fine of no more than $5 million for an individual and no more than $25 million for a defendant other than an individual. A reference to "10 years to life" means a term of imprisonment of not less than 10 years nor more than life. The Synthetic Drug Abuse Prevention Act of 2012—Subtitle D of Title XI of the Food and Drug Administration Safety and Innovation Act (P.L. 112-144)—added "cannabimimetic agents" to Schedule I of the Controlled Substances Act and defined such term to mean one of five structural classes of synthetic cannabinoids (and their analogues). Synthetic cannabinoid products are sometimes referred to as "synthetic marijuana," "Spice," or "K2." The act also added 11 synthetic stimulants and hallucinogens to Schedule I, including methylene dioxypyrovalerone (MDPV), a chemical ingredient found in designer drugs commonly referred to as "bath salts." The criminal penalties applicable to unlawful trafficking of these synthetic drugs are the same as those described below the "Any other Schedule I substance" table rows. In addition, any offense listed in this report that refers to "all substances" now encompasses these synthetic drugs. Finally, because these particular synthetic drugs are now regulated as controlled substances, the simple possession statute and its associated penalties, 21 U.S.C. 844, applies to them.

[2] 1 kilogram is equal to 35.27 ounces; 1 gram is equal to 0.04 ounces.

[3] Unlike the penalties for manufacturing, distribution, dispensing, or possession, those for importation or exportation do not distinguish between quantities of marihuana plants in excess of 100. Importation or exportation of any marihuana plants in excess of 100 is subject to higher penalties than those for less than 50 kilograms of marihuana, etc.

[4] Except in the case of 50 or more marihuana plants regardless of weight, and except that under section 841(b)(4) distribution of a small amount of marihuana for no remuneration is treated as a simple possession offense and punished under section 844, infra.

[5] Importation or exportation of any quantity of flunitrazepam is subject to a fine of $1/5 million and up to 20 years imprisonment.

[6] Id.

[7] Id.

[8] A second offense is one committed after a prior conviction for a felony drug offense has become final.

[9] See supra note 3.

[10] Except in the case of 50 or more marihuana plants regardless of weight and except that distribution of a small amount of marihuana is punishable as simple possession under section 844, infra.

[11] See supra note 5.

[12] Creating a serious hazard to human or animal life, or harming the environment, or causing water pollution as a result of using poisons, chemicals or other hazardous substances on Federal property while in the course of unlawfully manufacturing or otherwise distributing a controlled substance

[13] Possession with intent to use for unauthorized manufacture of a controlled substance; possession or distribution knowing that the chemical will be used for unauthorized manufacture of a controlled substance; or, with intent of causing evasion of the record-keeping or reporting requirements of 21 U.S.C. 830 (or regulations pursuant thereto), receipt or distribution of a reportable amount in units small enough so that the making of records or filing of reports is not required.

[14] "Date rape drug" means gamma hydroxybutyric acid (GHB) or any controlled substance analogue of GHB, including gamma butyrolactone (GBL) or 1,4-butanediol; ketamine; flunitrazepam; or any substance which the Attorney General designates, through a rulemaking proceeding, to be used in committing rape or sexual assault. 21 U.S.C. 841(g)(2)(A).

[15] Examples of prohibited activities include knowingly or intentionally: (1) delivering, distributing, or dispensing a controlled substance by means of the Internet by an online pharmacy that is not validly registered with the Drug Enforcement Administration (DEA); (2) writing a prescription for a controlled substance for the purpose of delivery, distribution, or dispensation by means of the Internet; (3) serving as an agent, intermediary, or other entity that causes the Internet to be used to bring together a buyer and seller to engage in such distribution; (4) offering to fill a prescription for a controlled substance based solely on a consumer's completion of an online medical questionnaire; and (5) making a material false, fictitious, or fraudulent statement or representation on the homepage of Internet sites operated by an online pharmacy regarding the pharmacy's compliance with federal and state controlled substance laws. 21 U.S.C. 841(h)(2).

[16] See pages 1-5 of this report for these penalties, which vary by type of substance, weight or other factual circumstances, and repeat offender status. 21 U.S.C. 841(h)(4).

[17] Knowingly distributing a controlled substance to an unauthorized person by a registrant, removing required labels, unlawful use of information acquired during a controlled substance inspection, failing to keep required records, etc. For more information about these federal requirements pertaining to the lawful handling of controlled substances, see CRS Report RL34635, The Controlled Substances Act: Regulatory Requirements, by James E. Nichols and Brian T. Yeh.

[18] To knowingly: use fictitious, revoked, suspended or expired registration number; obtain a controlled substance by fraud, forgery, or other form of deceit; provide false information; use labels and other markings to render a drug a counterfeit substance; unlawfully possess certain controlled substance manufacturing equipment; being a registrant, unlawfully distribute a controlled substance in the course of legitimate business; create or receive a mixture containing listed chemicals to evade regulatory requirements.

[19] Knowingly placing in any newspaper, magazine, handbill, or other publications, any written advertisement that has the purpose of seeking or offering illegally to receive, buy, or distribute a schedule I controlled substance. 21 U.S.C. 843(c). However, this offense does not include any advertisement that merely advocates the use of a schedule I controlled

substance and does not attempt to propose or facilitate an actual transaction in a schedule I controlled substance. Id. The Ryan Haight Online Pharmacy Consumer Protection Act of 2008, P.L. 110-425, creates an additional advertisement offense, new subsection 21 U.S.C. 843(c)(2): knowingly or intentionally using the Internet to advertise the sale of, or to offer to sell, distribute, or dispense a controlled substance in a manner that is not authorized by federal controlled substances law, including directing prospective buyers to online pharmacies that are not registered with the DEA. The penalties for the offense are the same as those for advertising in printed publications.

[20] Except that violation carries a mandatory minimum of no less than one year unless the offense involves marihuana in an amount of 5 grams or less.

[21] The offense includes distribution or manufacturing in or on, or within 1,000 feet of the real property comprising a public or private elementary, vocational, or secondary school or a public or private college, junior college, or university, or a playground, or housing facility owned by a public housing authority, or within 100 feet of a public or private youth center, public swimming pool, or video arcade facility.

[22] Also, at least twice any term of supervised released otherwise authorized for a first offense. An exception to the mandatory 1-year minimum is provided with respect to an offense involving 5 grams or less of marihuana. Where the statute provides for a different mandatory penalty, the higher prevails.

[23] If convicted of a simple possession offense, the defendant is required, if able, to pay the "reasonable costs" of the investigation and prosecution of the offense. Penalties for simple possession are also applicable to distribution of a "small amount" of marihuana for no remuneration.

[24] For purposes of the section under which the possession penalties are imposed, a prior conviction includes conviction of any offense under the Controlled Substances Act or the Controlled Substances Import and Export Act and any drug or narcotic offense chargeable under state law.

[25] Distributing a controlled substance to another with the intent to commit a crime of violence upon the victim.

[26] Assembly, maintenance, or placement—in connection with the manufacture, distribution, or dispensing of a controlled substance.

[27] Under the statute, a person is considered to be engaged in a continuing criminal enterprise if (1) he commits any felony violation of the Controlled Substances Act or the Controlled Substances Import and Export Act, (2) the violation is a part of a continuing series of violations of those statutes (A) which are undertaken by the person in concert with five or more other persons with respect to whom such person occupies a position of organizer, a supervisory position, or any other position of management, and (B) from which such person obtains substantial income or resources. Note that some violations carry the death penalty as discussed supra.

[28] Except in the case of methamphetamine, where these provisions apply to any enterprise that grosses $5 million or more a year, or involves 200 times of the amount of controlled substances required under 21 U.S.C. 841.

[29] Also, at least twice any term of supervised release otherwise authorized for a first offense. Any higher mandatory penalty otherwise authorized for the offense would prevail.

[30] Also, at least three times any term of supervised release otherwise authorized for a first offense. Penalties for third and subsequent offenses are governed by 21 U.S.C. 841(b)(1)(A).

[31] The penalties listed for this offense apply in addition to the punishment provided for the drug trafficking crime.

[32] The Ultralight Aircraft Smuggling Prevention Act of 2012, P.L. 112-93, expanded the liability for this offense to include anyone who attempts or conspires to commit aviation smuggling, thus subjecting them to the same penalties as those who commit the crime. In addition, this law added a definition of "aircraft" to include ultralight vehicles which meet the characteristics described in 14 C.F.R. 103.1. Such ultralight vehicles (operated by a single occupant and weighing less than 254 pounds) have reportedly been used by drug traffickers to cross the Mexico-U.S. border in their effort to smuggle the drugs into the United States. See Aaron Cooper, Gabrielle Giffords' Anti-Drug Legislation Signed into Law, Feb. 10, 2012, CNN, at http://articles.cnn.com/2012-02-10/politics/politics_giffords-ultralight-law_1_ultralights-traffickers-gabrielle-giffords?_s=PM:POLITICS.

INDEX

A

B

C

D

H

I

J

L

M

N

O

P

Q

R

S

T

U

V

W

Y